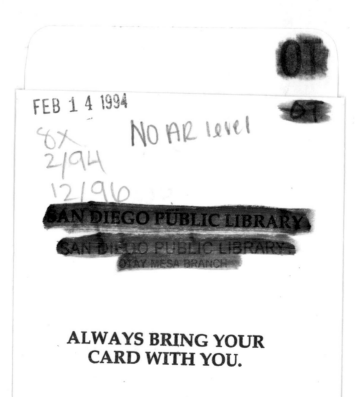

Sir Francis Drake

THE WORLD'S GREAT EXPLORERS

Francis Drake

WITHDRAWN

By Roberta Bard

Consultant: James Casada, Ph.D., Professor of History,
Winthrop College, Rock Hill, South Carolina

CHILDRENS PRESS®
CHICAGO

The crumbling Spanish fort at Portobello, Panama, near Nombre de Dios. Drake died and was buried at sea in this bay.

Dedicated to my husband, Warren Ruby, who understands the Armada, and to Thomas Kernan, my sixth-grade teacher at Stillman School, Tenafly, New Jersey, who made history exciting.

Project Editor: Ann Heinrichs
Designer: Lindaanne Donohoe
Cover Art: Steven Gaston Dobson
Engraver: Liberty Photoengraving

**Library of Congress
Cataloging-in-Publication Data**

Bard, Roberta.
  Francis Drake / by Roberta Bard.
    p. cm. — (The World's great explorers)
  Includes bibliographical references (p.) and index.
  Summary: Describes the life and adventures of the seaman who was the first Englishman to sail around the world.
  ISBN 0-516-03067-1
  1. Drake, Francis, Sir, 1540?-1596—Juvenile literature. 2. Great Britain—History, Naval—Tudors, 1485-1603—Juvenile literature. 3. America—Discovery and exploration—English—Juvenile literature. 4. Admirals—Great Britain—Biography—Juvenile literature. 5. Explorers—America—Biography—Juvenile literature. [1. Drake, Francis, Sir, 1540?-1596. 2. Explorers. 3. Admirals.] I. Title. II. Series.

DA86.22.D7R83 1992   91-34522
942.05'5'092—dc20   CIP
[B]   AC

Drake's fireships setting the Spanish Armada ablaze in 1588.

Table of Contents

Chapter 1
The Dragon Strikes

The Spanish galleon lay anchored near Calais, France, across the narrow English Channel from the coast of England. It was a little after midnight and the tide had just turned, flooding back toward the ships. The sailor on watch idly observed the ripples coming toward him. Nothing else moved in the silent dark.

Nearby he could see the *San Martin*, the great flagship of the Duke of Medina Sidonia, commander of the Invincible Armada. The rest of the fleet was gathered around, lanterns glowing softly on the decks.

The battle to bring England back to the Catholic Church and under Spain's control had been raging for days. Surely tomorrow God would deliver the English fleet into their hands. Elizabeth, the heretic Protestant queen, and Francis Drake, her pirate, who had dared to burn Cadiz harbor, would be destroyed. Spain would have vengeance for the damage Drake had done.

The Spanish sailor scanned the horizon, trying to separate sky from sea. Was that a darker place? a spot that didn't belong? Could something be out there? As he strained his eyes to see, the dark shape separated itself from the blackness around it.

A ghost ship, without a single light, but under full sail.

And another.

And another.

Eight dark ships moved in perfect rhythm in the midnight sea.

Suddenly the horizon was on fire. Eight ships blazed fiery red against the black sky.

He could see their crews silhouetted against the light. They were not fleeing from the burning ships. The crews were moving purposefully amid the flames. The ships were racing on the tide directly toward the Spanish fleet. Fireships! Hell-burners!

The Spanish watchman screamed the alarm, but by then the Armada could not intercept. The flaming ships were too close to the giant galleons, and the tide brought them closer each second.

The flames reached the fireships' loaded guns, exploding one after the other. Meanwhile, the smoke-blackened English crews jumped into longboats and rowed back to their fleet. But the Spaniards had no way of knowing that there was no one on board to aim the guns.

To the Spaniards who had awakened to see ships of fire coming at them, it seemed as if the devil had brought a fleet from hell to fight them. They cut the cables to their anchors and tried to escape on the tide. Great ships swung out of control and smashed into each other, crushing the hulls.

Only Medina Sidonia, the commander of the Armada, kept his head. He maneuvered his ship clear of the entangled galleons and blazing fireships. His escape route was open. Instead, he dropped anchor and fired his guns as a signal for the Armada to form

The first shot is fired against the Spanish Armada.

around him. It was the act of a good seaman and a brave man. But no one was listening. Most of his ships were heading eastward as fast as they could, away from the danger of fire. All around him floated pieces of charred and broken ships. The huge galleass named the *San Lorenzo* had run aground and lay on its side, its guns pointing helplessly up to heaven and down into the sand.

From the deck of his ship across the channel, a short, stocky Englishman watched the destruction with satisfaction. *El Draque*—the Dragon, Sir Francis Drake—had struck again.

Chapter 2
Early Life

Eight-year-old Francis Drake listened to the creaks of the wood and the lap of the water against the ship that was his new home. This ship wasn't going anywhere ever again. It wasn't even a whole ship—just the bottom part— and it was firmly grounded in the sands of the Medway, the river where the English navy usually anchored.

Francis didn't know it then, but he would live the rest of his life on ships. He would be the first Englishman to sail around the world. He would change the map of the earth. He would bring home treasure such as England had never dreamed of, and he would break the power of mighty Spain forever.

Francis hadn't always lived in the ship. He was born in his grandparents' cottage on Crowndale Farm near Plymouth, on the southern coast of England. He was probably born in 1540 or 1541, but there is no record of the month or year of his birth or of his mother's name. He was the oldest of twelve sons of Edmund Drake, a strong believer in the new Protestant religion. This Protestant faith was directly responsible for the family's unusual new home.

King Henry VIII

Martin Luther

Francis was born in a time when the Roman Catholic Church was a major political as well as religious power. In 1517, a young German priest named Martin Luther had protested against the church's wealth when so many people were poor, and against selling spiritual favors called indulgences. He wanted the Catholic Church to reform. Instead, his following of protesters grew, and the Protestant Reformation swept across Europe.

England, like the rest of Europe, was torn by the divisions in the Christian church. But King Henry VIII's personal struggles against the church made England's troubles even worse.

Anne Boleyn, the second wife of Henry VIII

Henry became king in 1509 when his older brother died. He married his brother's widow, Catherine of Aragon, a Spanish princess. Only one of their five children lived, a daughter named Mary. Henry wanted a son to rule after him. When the Catholic Church refused to grant Henry a divorce, he declared that the pope, the head of the church, had no authority in England. He married Anne Boleyn in 1533.

Henry VIII encouraged the English Parliament to pass several new laws. One law, the Act of Supremacy, decreed that the king was the head of the church in England. To question the king's authority over the church would be treason.

Jane Seymour, the third wife of Henry VIII

Henry VIII took away the Catholic Church's lands in England and gave them to his supporters. It was a good political move. People who received land had a strong reason to stay Protestant and support him. They would not want the Catholic Church to return to power. The king gave the abbey of Tavistock to John Russell, the earl of Bedford. These lands included Crowndale Farm, where Francis Drake was born.

King Henry still needed a son, but Anne Boleyn bore him a daughter, Elizabeth. He beheaded Anne and in 1536 married Lady Jane Seymour, who died shortly after the birth of a son, Edward. Henry married three more times but did not have any more children.

Nine-year-old Edward became King Edward VI when Henry died in 1547. The sickly young boy ruled for only six years. During his short reign, Protestantism became firmly established as the state religion. In 1549 the Church of England's *Book of Common Prayer* was published, and churches were required to use it in their services. The "idolatrous rite of the Mass" and the Catholic form of communion were forbidden.

Though England was officially a Protestant country, many people still considered themselves Catholic. Throughout the country, English Catholics rebelled. At Tavistock, the feeling ran so high that Lord Russell was sent home by the king to restore order. Russell, however, could not get any closer than fifty miles (eighty kilometers) away.

Protestant refugees hastened to the big city of Plymouth for safety. Among them were Edmund Drake and his family, including eight-year-old Francis. Tradition says they camped on an island in Plymouth Harbor. Nearly five hundred years later, it still has the nickname Drake's Island.

But Plymouth was not a safe place either. Many Plymouth residents were farmers and other workers who had been forced off the church lands. Unemployment, coupled with inflation and general social unrest, drove citizens to rebel. Rioting became so serious that a squadron of ships was sent to restore order.

Edmund Drake decided to move his family across the country to Kent, in southeastern England. There he found an old abandoned ship where he could raise his sons. Many of Francis's younger brothers were born on that ship. Edmund worked as a chaplain for the navy. Later he became the vicar of Upchurch in Kent.

The Drake family was poor. The boy got little book learning, but he could read and write. His father probably taught him to read the Bible. Francis didn't write particularly well, but he could speak well and give a good sermon. There are records of some of the speeches he later gave in the English Parliament, and they are strong and clear.

In 1553, as Francis was entering his teens, King Edward died at the age of sixteen. Mary, the Catholic daughter of Catherine of Aragon and Henry VIII, became queen. Mary had seen her mother deeply wronged by her father. She was determined to bring England back to the Catholic faith. She repealed all the religious laws of Edward's reign and revived severe laws against heresy. (Protestant beliefs that were different from the Catholic Church's teachings were considered heresy.) Over three hundred Protestant men and women were burned at the stake. There was so much religious persecution that she became known as Bloody Mary.

Mary, who was half Spanish, married Philip of Spain. The marriage infuriated her subjects, who saw Spain as England's great enemy. Mary reigned for five years and died in 1558. Her half-sister, the Protestant Elizabeth, then came to the throne.

During these years, when Francis was about fourteen, his father sent him to work for the master of a small ship that traded between England and Zeeland. (Zeeland, bordering the North Sea east of England, is now part of The Netherlands.) The owner of the ship was a bachelor who had no children. In his service, Francis learned the currents and shoals and sandbanks of the English Channel and the North Sea. There would come a time when his country would depend for its very existence on the knowledge he was

King Edward VI

ANNO DNI · I S 4 4
LADI MARI DOVGHTER TO
THE MOST VERTVOVS PRINC
KINGE HENRI THE EIGHT
THE AGE OF · XXVIII YERES

Queen Mary I of England

acquiring about these waters. When the old bachelor died, he left the little ship to Francis.

The seafaring world that Francis Drake entered had changed dramatically in the preceding decades, thanks to explorers such as Christopher Columbus and Ferdinand Magellan. Europeans at that time were hungry for spices, dyes, and textiles from faraway Asian lands known as the Indies. Merchants transported these goods overland by caravan through hostile territories. As a result, these trade goods were very expensive, but people were willing to pay huge prices for them. If merchants could find a way to sail to the Indies, they could bring in more goods at a lower cost and thus reap greater profits.

Prince Henry the Navigator

Portugal took the lead in sea exploration, encouraged by Prince Henry the Navigator. Before his death in 1460, Henry sent out more than fifty expeditions to explore the African coast.

Christopher Columbus, a sailor from Genoa, Italy, got most of his seafaring knowledge and experience from working for the Portuguese. Columbus was a serious student of geography. He wrote to geographers and he read the travel book of Marco Polo, a thirteenth-century adventurer from Venice who traveled to China.

Like many other geographers of the time, Columbus thought the earth was smaller than it is. Sailors and educated men believed the earth was round, but they underestimated its size. They believed the ocean between Europe and Asia was fairly narrow, no more than three or four thousand miles across. They had no suspicion that the American continents existed.

Convinced that he could sail westward from Europe to the Indies, Columbus took his ideas to the king of Portugal. But the Portuguese were busy exploring an eastward route to the Indies by sailing around Africa. They were not interested in a westward route.

Columbus next went to Spain and appealed to Queen Isabella to support his expedition, but he had to wait several years before she responded. For centuries, Spain had been fighting the Moors, Muslim invaders from North Africa. Queen Isabella and King Ferdinand wanted to unite Spain under the Catholic Church and exclude all non-Christians. As part of that effort, they created the Spanish Inquisition. This was a special court that tried, imprisoned, and killed people suspected of not holding Catholic beliefs. The Inquisition existed for over three hundred years and was very active during Drake's time.

Columbus and Queen Isabella

In 1492, the Spaniards finally drove the last of the Moors out of Spain. That same year, Spain's Jews were also expelled. Now Isabella had time to listen to Columbus. She agreed to pay for an expedition of three ships and gave Columbus authority over any lands he might discover in the name of Spain.

Columbus expected to go to the Indies. Instead, he found a whole new world not shown on European maps. He made four voyages exploring the Caribbean islands and the coasts of Central and South America. Still believing he had found the Indies, he called the New World natives Indians. Eventually the Caribbean region came to be known as the West Indies.

Spain and Portugal soon made sweeping and conflicting claims as a result of their discoveries. They referred their dispute to the pope for arbitration. He made a Line of Demarcation—an imaginary north-south line about 300 miles (480 kilometers) west of the Azores and Cape Verde Islands. It extended around the globe to the eastern hemisphere. Spain was granted rights to all newly discovered lands west of the line, and Portugal had rights to lands east of it. In 1494, Spain and Portugal agreed to move the line even farther west.

Portugal continued its explorations to the east. By 1498, Portuguese navigators had sailed around the southern tip of Africa all the way to India. In 1500, a Portuguese fleet bound for India blew off its course and found the coast of Brazil. Portugal was able to claim it because Brazil was east of the line. The rest of South America went to Spain.

Portugal eventually conquered parts of Africa, India, Ceylon, Malaya, and the islands of the Moluccas— better known in Europe as the Spice Islands.

Map showing the Line of Demarcation that divided the world between Spain and Portugal

Vasco Núñez de Balboa

Ferdinand Magellan

Spanish explorers, meanwhile, investigated the New World. In 1513, a Spaniard named Vasco Núñez de Balboa crossed the Isthmus of Panama and looked out on a great ocean. Because of the way the land curves, the Pacific Ocean is south of the Atlantic at that point. Balboa called the Pacific the South Sea and claimed it for Spain. Drake, too, would one day gaze upon this great South Sea and vow to sail upon it.

In 1519, Ferdinand Magellan, a Portuguese navigator sailing for Spain, proved it was possible to sail all the way around the world. He sailed across the Atlantic, down the coast of South America to its southern tip, and through a passageway that is named for him, the Strait of Magellan. He found himself in the same great ocean that Balboa saw. It looked so peaceful that he named it the Pacific, from the Latin word for peaceful. Magellan was killed near the Philippine Islands. But one ship and eighteen crew members survived to complete the voyage and return to Spain. The next person to circumnavigate the world would be Francis Drake.

By Drake's time, Spain controlled the West Indies, Central America, and South America except for Brazil. With their superior technology—horses and guns—the Spaniards overcame the Aztecs in Mexico and the Incas in South America. Viceroys, or representatives of the king, ruled the Spanish colonies.

Soon a steady stream of treasure was flowing from the mines of South America across the Atlantic to the royal coffers. This treasure made Spain the most powerful country in Europe. Spain made laws that said all silver and gold from the New World had to be shipped in Spanish ships to the port of Seville in Spain. Foreigners were barred from Spanish colonies.

The other European nations had no intention of being frozen out of the New World's wealth. They encouraged pirates to attack the treasure ships. In violation of Spanish law, they traded with the colonists, sending them goods that Spain couldn't supply.

In England, there appeared a new breed of sea captain, part trader and part pirate. The English called them "sea dogs." The sea dogs ignored Spanish laws. They sailed and traded wherever they chose. They attacked Spanish ships, captured their treasure, and brought it back to England. They challenged the might of Spain and helped England become a major power.

One of the best sea dogs was a man named John Hawkins, who owned a prosperous shipping company in Plymouth. He was a distant kinsman of Francis Drake. When Francis was about twenty years old, he sold his little bark and went to work for John Hawkins.

Sir John Hawkins

Chapter 3
San Juan de Ulúa

John Hawkins's shipping business was active in the slave trade to Spanish colonies in the New World. In the 1400s, as Portugal explored the coast of West Africa, it began to ship Africans to Europe as slaves. The slavery business expanded when Spain started colonies in Central and South America.

Slavery had been a fact of life in Europe and the Middle East for centuries. It was especially prevalent during the Crusades, the Christian military campaigns against Muslims. Christian prisoners rowed the galleys of Muslim warships, and Muslim prisoners were galley slaves on Christian ships.

Because they were Protestants, English seamen who were captured by Spaniards were tried before the Spanish Inquisition. If they were not executed, they were often enslaved in the galleys or sent to the mines. Slavery existed in Africa, too. Africans enslaved others they captured in intertribal warfare.

In the New World, a constant supply of labor was needed to work the land and the mines. Europeans sickened and died from the harsh climate and hard working conditions. The native Indians could not be controlled. From the early years of the colonies, Spaniards bought African slaves. Spain believed in government control of the slave trade and granted licenses to only a few suppliers. The result was that slaves were hard to get and the price was high.

John Hawkins knew that Spaniards would buy slaves from him. He wanted a license from the Spanish government. He was a good businessman and, by the standards of those times, he behaved honestly. In 1562 and 1564, Hawkins made two successful voyages selling slaves to Spanish colonists in the New World. He did not engage in piracy, as French adventurers were doing. But King Philip of Spain was determined not to allow English Protestants to do business in his colonies. Instead of granting a license, he sent orders that Hawkins was to be treated as a pirate.

Hawkins had made friends with the Spanish colonists and some of the officials. They were eager to trade with him despite the official orders. He made plans for another voyage in 1566. Unable to go himself, he appointed Captain John Lovell to be in command. Young Francis Drake joined the venture.

Lovell was not as skilled a trader as Hawkins. He took the Africans to South America's northern coast, called the Spanish Main, visiting the same towns where Hawkins had gone. One town was Rio de la Hacha, a seaport on the northwest coast of present-day Colombia. There the Spanish governor, Miguel de Castellanos, tricked Lovell into landing ninety Africans and then refused to pay for them.

Hawkins did not employ Lovell again. He led the next big expedition himself. He took his young kinsman Drake with him as an officer on his flagship, the *Jesus of Lübeck*.

The *Jesus* was a huge 700-ton ship that was lent by Queen Elizabeth. It was beautiful to behold, like a floating castle, but it was old and rotten. Four days into the voyage, the little fleet ran into a gale and the *Jesus* nearly sank. This lesson had important conse-

Today's residents of Punta Alegre, a village on the Gulf of Panama, are descendants of slaves brought from Africa.

quences. Both Drake and Hawkins learned that the old-style battleships were not good for ocean sailing. Many years later, Hawkins would remember this and favor low-built, easily handled ships when he redesigned England's navy.

Hawkins sailed along the coast of Africa, but he collected only about 150 slaves, not enough to justify crossing the Atlantic. An African king asked him for help against another king and offered him the prisoners as payment. Hawkins helped in the attack and took several hundred prisoners for his cargo.

After leaving Africa, Hawkins put Drake in charge of the 50-ton *Judith*. This was Drake's first independent command. They visited several Spanish ports and did a profitable trade. All the governors ignored the orders from King Philip. To make things look right, they usually arranged for Hawkins to threaten to capture the town. The ship would fire guns overhead, being careful not to hit anyone. Then the governor could write to his superiors in Spain that he had been forced to surrender.

Hawkins sent Drake ahead in the *Judith* to Rio de la Hacha, where Lovell had left slaves and not been paid. Drake did not intend to be tricked again by Governor Castellanos. He demanded leave to fill his water caskets.

When Castellanos refused and opened fire, Drake sent shots at Castellanos's house. It was a hotheaded thing to do, but Drake had a temper. However, he did not have enough men to finish the job, and he had to wait for Hawkins. While he was waiting, a Spanish caravel came into the harbor. Drake chased and captured it right under Castellanos's guns.

When Hawkins came, he landed two hundred men. He captured the town and threatened to burn it unless the governor allowed him to trade. The colonists wanted to buy slaves and English merchandise, and they forced Castellanos to give in.

Hawkins continued down the coast to Cartagena, the capital of the Spanish Main. It was a fortified city with five hundred soldiers. When the governor refused to let Hawkins trade, it was not a charade. He meant what he said. However, young Francis Drake had a chance to study the city's defenses. Eighteen years later he would use that knowledge against Spain.

The voyage was a success and it was time to return home. They had just enough food for a quick passage. But they were caught in a heavy gale off Cuba. Once again, the *Jesus of Lübeck* nearly foundered. One of the sailors wrote, "the planks did open and shut with every sea, the seas without number and the leak so

big as the thickness of a man's arm, the living fish did swim upon the ballast as in the sea." Clearly, the *Jesus* was in no condition to cross the ocean.

Hawkins had a ticklish situation. The *Jesus of Lübeck* belonged to the queen. The financial arrangements were that if the ship needed repairs the investors had to pay for them, but if it sank, the whole loss would be the queen's. The sensible thing was to transfer the treasure and let the ship sink. But Hawkins was determined that the queen's ship would not sink under his command.

A galleon in the harbor of Cartagena, Colombia, now used as a restaurant

Hawkins asked advice from a Spanish ship captain. The captain advised him that the nearest port where he could make repairs was San Juan de Ulúa, on an island off the coast of Mexico.

There was a small problem. San Juan de Ulúa happened to be the port where the Spanish treasure fleet came once a year to pick up the bullion from the Mexican mines and transport it back to Spain. The fleet was due any day. Meeting up with this fleet would be almost the same as meeting up with King Philip himself.

Hawkins decided he had to take the risk. His ship carried a British flag, but it was so worn from the weather that the Spanish officials in San Juan de Ulúa could not tell whether it was a French or an English flag.

Before the Spaniards realized it was an English fleet, Hawkins slipped past them into the port. That was the last of his good luck. Two days later the treasure fleet arrived. On board was Don Martin Enriquez, the new viceroy of Mexico, the direct representative of King Philip.

Hawkins took control of the island that guarded the approach to the harbor. But he knew that if he tried to keep the Spanish fleet out of the harbor it would be an act of war. He opened negotiations with the viceroy to find a way for both fleets to use the harbor.

The viceroy was also in trouble. He was the ruler of Mexico. To take orders from an English sea captain was intolerable. But he could not win in battle because Hawkins controlled the island. If he negotiated, though, he might be rebuked by the king for making deals with a pirate.

Don Martin held a council. The council agreed to accept Hawkins's terms until the fleet was safely berthed in the San Juan port. Then they would attack. The viceroy did not see anything wrong with this action. As a Spanish nobleman, he saw no reason to honor an agreement with an English pirate.

Hawkins demanded that both sides exchange hostages of high rank as a pledge of good faith. Since the Spaniards were planning on treachery, they were sure their hostages would be killed. They decided to send ten common sailors in officers' clothing. But the common sailors did not want the job, and it was feared they would give the plot away. Ten brave Spanish gentlemen volunteered to take the assignment, including the vice admiral, Captain Ubillo.

The agreement was made—no hostilities, ten hostages on each side. Hawkins would hold the island and no armed Spaniards would land on it. Hawkins would repair his ships and make proper payment for food and supplies.

The Spanish ships passed peacefully into the harbor. What Hawkins did not know was that the viceroy had sent for all the soldiers in the nearby town of Veracruz. They had boarded the ships the night before. In the harbor the viceroy called another council to make the final plans.

Hawkins did not trust the Spaniards, but he thought he had protected himself because he controlled the island and the roadway to Veracruz. He got suspicious when he saw gunports being cut in one of the Spanish merchantmen. He sent his ship's master, Robert Barrett, who spoke Spanish, to investigate. As soon as Barrett arrived on the ship, the viceroy took him prisoner.

When Hawkins sat down to dinner with his Spanish hostages, an alert young steward discovered that one of the hostages had a knife up his sleeve. Hawkins and his men raced for the upper deck. A trumpet call went out from the Spanish flagship, and Spanish soldiers and sailors poured forth from their hiding places. All the Englishmen on the island were killed except for three who were able to swim to the *Jesus of Lübeck*. Another English ship, the *Minion*, was taken by the Spanish and retaken by Hawkins. The Spanish flagship sank in flames, but the water was so shallow it was still able to fight.

The Spanish captain, Ubillo, whose ship had been sunk, went ashore. He paid for the use of a ship, set it afire, and sent it toward the English. The crew of the *Minion* cut their cables and tried to work out to sea, away from the danger of fire.

Hawkins had only three ships left—the *Minion*, the *Jesus of Lübeck*, and Drake's little *Judith*. The *Jesus* could not be saved. The crew, the supplies, and the treasure were transferred to the two smaller ships. Hawkins stayed aboard until the very last moment and then leaped to the deck of the *Minion* as it pulled away. He did not know that his eleven-year-old nephew, Paul, who had served him as a page, was still on the *Jesus*. The Spaniards captured the boy, and many years later he married a wealthy Mexican woman.

With the new day came strong winds. Hawkins lost three anchors and two cables in the storm. Drake and the *Judith* had vanished. Hawkins was angry and said later that "they forsook us in our great misery." However, Drake had a small ship and he could not have helped the *Minion*. In fact, he may have thought Hawkins had forsaken him.

The *Minion*'s trip home was a nightmare. Hawkins had two hundred men on board and could not feed them. One hundred asked to be put ashore and risk capture by the Spaniards rather than face a slow death by starvation. Those who stayed on board ate dogs, cats, rats, and parrots. Only fifteen were still alive when they reached England. Drake had arrived just five days earlier in the *Judith*.

The *Minion* and the *Judith* carried enough gold, silver, and pearls that it took four pack horses to carry the loot back to London. But the expedition had been a disaster. They lost three ships, and of the four hundred men who sailed from Plymouth, only seventy came home.

Drake never forgot or forgave what happened at San Juan de Ulúa. For the rest of his life Spain was his enemy, and he was determined to make Spain pay for its treachery.

A storm-bashed ship in trouble

Chapter 4
The Raid on Nombre de Dios

In July 1569, Francis Drake married Mary Newman, a seaman's daughter from a town near Plymouth. But he did not stay home on land for long. In 1570 and 1571 he made two voyages. His purpose was to gather information that might help him get revenge for the disaster at San Juan de Ulúa. On the second of these voyages, he set up a secret hideaway he called Port Pheasant on the Spanish Main. Port Pheasant, he knew, would be useful to him on a future voyage. He was particularly interested in Nombre de Dios, a city on the Atlantic coast of present-day Panama. Twice a year, all the treasure from the mines of Peru and Mexico came to Nombre de Dios to be loaded onto ships and taken to Spain. In 1572, Drake returned to the New World to capture that treasure and bring it home to England.

We know about this voyage because several of the sailors kept journals or made reports. Their records were combined into a narrative. Before his death, Drake reviewed it and added his own notes and comments. Then in 1626, Drake's nephew (also named Francis Drake) published the narrative, entitled *Sir Francis Drake Revived*. This nephew was the son of Thomas, Drake's youngest brother, and was the only surviving descendant of the twelve Drake brothers.

Drake took only two small ships, the 70-ton *Pascha* and his own little 25-ton *Swan*, which was captained by his brother John. The seventy-three crewmen were all young volunteers. Only one man was over thirty years old. The ships carried an unusual assortment of supplies—not only tools, munitions, and artillery, but also drums and trumpets, and "three dainty pinnaces made in Plymouth, taken asunder all in pieces and stowed aboard, to be set up as occasion served." (Quotations here are from *Sir Francis Drake Revived*, with the spellings of words modernized.)

Pinnaces were light, open boats that would sail well, row easily, and operate in shallow water where no ship was able to follow them. These practical little boats played an important part in Drake's plans.

On July 12, 1572, after an easy ocean crossing, the *Pascha* and the *Swan* sailed into Drake's secret hideaway, Port Pheasant. The supplies and arms he had hidden there before were gone. A fire was burning in a great tree trunk, and a message written on a lead plate was nailed to another tree.

"Captain Drake, if you fortune to come into this port, make haste away: For the Spaniards which you had with you here last year have betrayed this place, and taken away all that you left here. I depart from thence this present 7 of July, 1572. Your very loving friend, John Garrett."

The warning was just five days old. Drake had to make a quick decision. The smart thing would be to leave at once. But he had to have a home base, and Port Pheasant was perfect for his plans to attack Nombre de Dios. A new place might not be any safer. He set one group of men to work putting the pinnaces together and another group building a stockade.

A view on the Spanish Main

The next day another visitor came to their not-so-secret harbor. This time it was an English ship commanded by Captain James Rance. Some of his crew had sailed with Drake the year before and knew about the harbor. Since Rance had seen the stockade and the pinnaces, there was no point in trying to hide their plans. Drake invited him to be a formal partner in the raid on the treasure.

The combined forces sailed to a small group of islands called the Isles of Pines, close to Nombre de Dios. There they met a group of African slaves who had been left to cut timber for their Spanish masters in Nombre de Dios. Drake talked to them and got some valuable information about groups of escaped slaves called Cimaroons. These were "a black people, which about 80 years past, fled from the Spaniards their masters, by reason of their cruelty, and are since grown to a nation, under two kings of their own," wrote one of the sailors. Every year some slaves managed to escape and join this group. Just six weeks earlier, the Cimaroons had almost taken Nombre de Dios in a surprise attack. The slaves said the governor of Panama was expected to send reinforcements to the Spaniards any day.

Drake had counted on the element of surprise in his attack. Now he knew Nombre de Dios was on the alert and would soon be strongly defended. He had to move fast.

At the slaves' request, Drake took them to the mainland where they could join the Cimaroons. Then he outfitted fifty of his men and twenty of Rance's men for battle, giving them muskets, bows, and fire-pikes—flame-bearing spears to use in close action. Four sailors received drums and trumpets. The crew rowed to Nombre de Dios in the pinnaces and hid, waiting for dawn when they planned to attack.

That night Drake overheard his men talking. They had heard too much from the slaves about the strength of the town. Morale was dropping fast. Drake thought the best cure was action. As soon as the moon began to rise, Drake calmly lied and announced that it was the sun rising and it was time to attack.

The pinnaces sped silently across the bay toward the city, but luck was against them. Just then a Spanish ship laden with wine from the Canary Islands sailed into the bay. The alert master saw them and immediately launched a boat to give warning.

Drake steered between the boat and the shore, landing his sailors on a little spit of land. They raced for the gun platform that protected the town from attack by sea and tipped the cannon off the platform. The lone Spanish gunner fled. Quick as they were, it was too late. The alarm bell in the church tower was already clanging.

Drake split his small force into three parts. One group stayed to guard the pinnaces. The second force went with his brother John behind the king's treasure house to enter the market square. Drake himself led the third group down the main street with drums beating, trumpets blaring, and fire-pikes and flaming arrows spreading terror.

As they burst into the main square, a group of Spanish soldiers loosed a volley of fire. Drake's young trumpeter fell dead, the only casualty of the battle.

Drake felt a searing pain in his leg, but he gave no sign to his men that he had been shot. They fought the Spanish, first with muskets, then hand to hand. The Spaniards put up a brave defense until they heard English war cries behind them. John Drake had arrived with his men. Caught between the two forces, the Spaniards broke and ran.

Francis Drake forced two captured Spaniards to lead the way to the governor's house, where bars of silver were stored before being shipped to Spain. The rest of the treasure—gold, pearls, and jewels—was kept nearby in the king's treasure house.

The great door where the pack mules were unloaded was open, and by the light of a candle on the stairs they saw "a pile of bars of silver, of (as near as we could guess) seventy foot in length, of ten foot in breadth, and twelve foot in height, piled up against the wall."

The sailors rushed for the treasure, but Drake stopped them. He "commanded straightly that none of us should touch a bar of silver, . . . there was in the king's treasure house, near the water side, more gold and jewels than all our four pinnaces could carry." No one knows why Drake did not take the silver.

Drake now received an unexpected reward for his kindness to the slaves on the Isles of Pines. A black man named Diego came to the pinnaces asking for Captain Drake. He warned them that the governor of Panama had sent troops, so they had better be away from shore by daybreak.

Drake's men raced for the king's treasure house, where the gold was stored. Before they could break in, they were caught in a violent tropical storm. They crouched in the shelter of a shed at the end of the treasure house while torrents of rain soaked their bowstrings and matches and powder. Drake fumed and tried not to call attention to his wound. Some of his men began to mutter about the danger. Drake exploded, "I have brought you to the treasure house of the world. If you leave without it, you may henceforth blame nobody but yourselves."

A "long half hour" later, the rains finally died away. Drake called his men to follow him. He took a brisk step—and fell in a faint. The sailors saw that his footprints in the sand were crimson. They took off his boot and found it full of blood.

Portrait of Francis Drake with his signature, "Fra. Drake"

The treasure house was forgotten. They revived Drake with rum and bound his leg with a scarf to stop the blood. He insisted they should get on with the important work of looting, but they ignored his protests and carried him to the pinnaces by force. They told him that, while they "had him to command them, they might recover wealth sufficient; but if once they lost him, they should hardly be able to recover home."

A port on the Chagres River

The great raid on Nombre de Dios ended in failure. They had no silver, no gold, no jewels. The only booty they took was the wine from the ship that had warned the town.

Drake recovered quickly from his wound. While his leg was mending, he sent his brother John inland to explore the Chagres River. John reported that a pinnace could row upstream for three days and reach the little river port of Venta Cruces. Mule trains carried treasure from the mines of Peru through Venta Cruces on their way to Nombre de Dios. Drake filed this information away for later use. He had a different destination in mind for the treasure.

A week after the Nombre de Dios attack, Drake made a raid on Cartagena, the capital and crown jewel of the Spanish Main. Under cover of night, he led his three pinnaces right into Cartagena's well defended harbor. At the entrance they met an old Spanish sailor who was alone on a ship. The Spaniard was bored and glad to have company. He foolishly told them about a large ship with an empty hold in the next bay.

Drake and his men rowed over to inspect this nice prize. It was a lovely ship, more than 200 tons— nearly three times the size of Drake's largest ship, the *Pascha*. It dwarfed the little pinnaces. Drake and his sailors "forthwith boarded her" and locked the Spanish crew below in the hold. They attached the great ship to the three pinnaces and boldly towed it across the harbor, just out of range of the Spanish guns.

On the way home with their prize, they seized two more small ships. Drake probably enjoyed reading captured letters meant for the governor of Cartagena. They were reporting the attack on Nombre de Dios and warning the governor to be on the lookout for a Captain Drake.

After questioning his prisoners, he put them ashore. Unlike many of his contemporaries, Drake did not kill or mistreat prisoners.

One of his sailors reported that Drake and his men captured about 120 ships along the coast between Cartagena and Nombre de Dios, "some of them twice or thrice each" and "never burnt nor sunk any" unless they were warships or had been used as bait to trick them. "And of all the men taken . . . we let them also free." Letters written by Spanish prisoners confirm this account.

Drake now had a perplexing problem—too many ships and too few men. He came up with a radical solution—one that he had to keep secret because it would horrify his crew. He decided to burn one of his own ships and make the other a storehouse. Then he could use all his men as crews for the pinnaces in the next part of his plan. He needed to keep the *Pascha* because it was big enough to carry the entire crew when they returned to England. His own ship, the little *Swan*—captained by his own brother—would have to be the sacrifice.

Drake wanted the destruction of the *Swan* to look like an accident. He sent for Thomas Moone, the ship's carpenter, and asked him "to conceal for a time a piece of service." He ordered Moone to go down secretly into the well of the *Swan* in the middle of the night "and bore three holes as near to the keel as he could."

Thomas Moone was "utterly dismayed." He wanted to know why Drake would sink his own ship, "so goodly a bark . . . new and strong, and that . . . had been in two so rich and gainful voyages." He also had a perfectly reasonable fear that if the *Swan*'s captain, John Drake, and the rest of the company knew of Moone's part, "he thought verily they would kill him." Drake used all his charm, and Moone was persuaded.

Early the next morning, Francis Drake paddled over to the *Swan* and asked his brother John to go fishing with him. As they rowed away, Francis just happened to mention how low the ship seemed to sit in the water.

John sent his steward to see if there was water in the hold. The steward went down in the hold and found himself waist-deep in water. John called all his crew to the pumps. Francis offered to help, but John said he had enough men and "let Francis carry on with his fishing."

When Francis came back at 3:00 that afternoon, it was clear the *Swan* could not be saved. He solemnly advised the men to burn the ship so that it could not fall into Spanish hands. He gave the command of the *Pascha* to John, and he moved to one of the pinnaces.

It must have hurt to sacrifice the *Swan*. But Drake had what he wanted—enough crew to man the three pinnaces, those wonderful boats that could be rowed up the Chagres River to Venta Cruces.

This time the great sea pirate planned to rob the Spanish treasure train on land.

Portrait of Francis Drake

Chapter 5
The Treasure Trains

Drake moved his men to a new hideout. Each day, half the men worked at clearing the jungle and building huts, while the other half played at sports—bowls, quoits, ninepins, and archery. Diego, the African who had warned them at Nombre de Dios, joined the company.

After two weeks, Drake left his brother John in charge of the camp, while he took two pinnaces and set out to make quick attacks along the coast. He wanted to keep the Spaniards' attention on the sea so they would not suspect a land attack on the treasure trains. Drake's custom was to take what he needed from the ships he attacked and send the ships and their crews safely on their way. Then he buried the stolen stores in hiding places up and down the coast.

One night Drake's party rowed the pinnaces up a river and moored them to a tree. There they faced a new enemy. One of the sailors reported "a monstrous shower of rain." After the storm "there came such an innumerable multitude of a kind of flies of that country called muskitos (like our gnats) which bite so spitefully that we could not rest all that night, nor find means to defend our selves from them." The best remedy they could find was "juice of lemons."

While Drake played hide-and-seek along the Spanish Main, his brother John made contact with the Cimaroons. When Drake came back, the two groups had a conference. The Cimaroons, who knew about the raid on Nombre de Dios, held Drake in high honor because he was an enemy of the Spaniards. They were "ready to assist and favour his enterprises against his and their enemies to the uttermost."

The Cimaroons were amazed to learn that Drake wanted to capture the Spanish gold. They thought gold was pretty but useless. They liked to steal it just to annoy the Spaniards. "Had they known gold had been his desire, they could have satisfied him," but the gold was buried under the flooded rivers of the rainy season. The Spaniards did not send their gold overland during the rainy season, either. Drake would have to wait five more months before he could attack the treasure trains.

After making more raids along the coast, Francis Drake and his men returned to their camp late in November. Terrible news awaited them. John Drake was dead, killed in a foolish raid. He had let the crew talk him into attacking a frigate while armed with only a rusty musket and a broken sword.

There was more tragedy to come. "About the beginning of January, half a score of our company fell down sick together, and the most of them died within two or three days." Men continued to sicken and die. Joseph Drake, another brother, died in Francis's arms. Drake ordered the surgeon to perform an autopsy. Most people of that time believed that dissecting a body was a sacrilege, an action against God. But Drake hoped this knowledge would save the rest of his men. A crew member wrote down the autopsy report. From the description, it appears that the crew probably had yellow fever, a disease carried by infected mosquitoes.

The surgeon who performed the autopsy died just a few days later, after making a powerful drug and testing it on himself. By the end of January, when the deaths finally ceased, Drake had lost twenty-eight men, or nearly half the crew.

Soon the Cimaroons reported that the treasure was moving. Mule trains laden with gold and silver were coming across Panama. Drake put Ellis Hixon in charge of the camp. He told Hixon not to believe any message unless it was in Drake's own handwriting. Then he took seventeen of his men and thirty Cimaroons and headed toward the distant town of Venta Cruces. Although they were in the tropics, the trees grew so tall and thick that the trip was cool and pleasant.

Pedro, the Cimaroon leader, promised to lead Drake to a place where he could see both the Atlantic and the Pacific, the vast secret ocean of Spain, at the same time. On February 11, 1573, after four days' march, Pedro, "the chiefest of these Cimaroons took our captain by the hand, and prayed him to follow him, if he was desirous to see at once the two seas, which he had so long longed for." Together they climbed "a great high tree" to a lookout platform.

For the first time Francis Drake saw the Pacific Ocean. He fell to his knees in prayer and "besought Almighty God of his goodness, to give him life and leave to sail once in an English ship in that sea." One of his men, John Oxenham, said that unless Drake "did beat him from his company, he would follow him by God's grace." From that moment on, Drake lived for the day when he could make his prayer come true and be the first Englishman to sail the Pacific.

Drake's first view of the Pacific

Three days later they arrived at Venta Cruces. A Cimaroon spy slipped into the city and came back with good news. The treasurer of Lima was traveling that very night with a treasure train of mules. Eight of them were laden with gold and one with jewels. Two other trains carried supplies and silver.

Drake set up an ambush. He hid his men in the long grass about fifty feet (fifteen meters) from the trail. The mules, fastened together one behind the other, were trained to lie down when the first mule lay down. Drake placed his men so his group could leap out and seize the lead mule of the first train and force it to lie down. John Oxenham and the Cimaroon captain would do the same with the lead mule of the second train. Drake told his men to wear their white shirts on the outside of their clothes. This would make

Mules are still used as pack animals in Central and South America. This is a small mule train in Guanajuato, Mexico.

them visible and keep them from attacking each other by mistake in the dark.

He warned the men not to show themselves or make any noise. He said to let any mules traveling *away* from Venta Cruces pass quietly because they were going the wrong direction and carried no gold.

Everyone obeyed, except one man.

Robert Pike had been drinking. One sailor's report says he had "drunken too much *aqua vitae* [alcohol] without water." Pike decided to be a hero. He sneaked forward in the grass, planning to grab the lead mule. When a rider passed by, coming from Venta Cruces, Pike rose up in the grass. One of the Cimaroons pulled him down and lay on top of him, but the white shirt was very visible in the darkness, and the rider had seen it. He put spurs to his horse and galloped away.

Drake heard the change in the hoofbeats. He suspected his plan had been discovered, but he didn't know why. He kept his men quietly in place. After all, the road was dangerous and the traveler might have sped up for his own reasons.

But the rider met the treasurer of Lima only a few miles away and reported what he had seen. The treasurer shrewdly sent the supply trains first instead of the treasure train. When Drake's men attacked the mule trains, they found no treasure. Even worse, they had given themselves away. The soldiers in Venta Cruces would soon know about the attack.

The Cimaroon captain told Drake there were only two ways he could go—back the long hard trip through the forest, or forward to Venta Cruces "and make a

Panama's Chagres River, as seen from the Trans-Isthmus Highway

way with his sword through the enemies." Drake chose the short route. They met one group of soldiers and had a brief battle just outside the city. One man died. Drake and another man were slightly wounded.

In one of the houses in Venta Cruces, they found three women who had come from Nombre de Dios to have their babies. Venta Cruces had a much more healthful climate and was safer for newborns. The Spanish women were terrified. Drake gave an order to all his men and the Cimaroons that "they should never hurt any woman, nor man that had not weapon in his hand to do them hurt." He visited the new mothers himself to assure them that they and their babies were safe. His men did not damage the town, but they were allowed to take any spoils that were not too heavy and would not interfere with fighting.

On the way back to the ship, the company camped for several days in a Cimaroon town so the exhausted men could let their feet heal after the long march. The Cimaroons were used to the climate and the terrain. Sometimes, when one of Drake's men had "fainted from sickness or weariness, two Cimaroons would carry him with ease between them two miles together."

From the Cimaroon settlement, Drake sent a message to Ellis Hixon, who had been taking care of the ship for the past three weeks. Hixon received the Cimaroon messenger courteously, but he followed orders and did not believe the message until the Cimaroon showed him Drake's gold toothpick where the captain had carved with a knife "By me Francis Drake." Hixon took the pinnace to the mouth of the river and rescued Drake and his men.

Once again they had returned without gold or other treasure.

Undaunted, Drake started planning a new attack. Cimaroon spies reported that mule trains were marching nightly to Nombre de Dios. Drake sent half his company with John Oxenham in the pinnace named the *Bear* to get food and supplies. The other half stayed to lie in wait for the ships carrying gold to Nombre de Dios. Oxenham's group captured a fine ship with twenty-eight hogs, two hundred hens, and a hold filled with corn. The ship was just what Drake needed to make the homeward voyage. He mounted guns on it and provisioned it.

He set sail with the new ship and the *Bear* toward Nombre de Dios. On the way, they met a French privateer, Captain Guillaume le Testu, who asked for water for his ship. When they anchored, le Testu gave Drake a gold scimitar—a curved sword—that had belonged to a king of France, as a thank-you gift. Drake in turn gave him a gold chain and medallion. Le Testu brought up-to-date news from Europe. He told them about a massacre of Protestants that took place in France on St. Bartholomew's Day. It no doubt brought back to Drake his memories of fleeing from home as a child because of religious persecution.

Le Testu wanted to join with Drake on this expedition. Drake didn't want a partner but saw no way out. Le Testu had an eighty-ton ship and seventy men. Drake had about thirty in his crew. He agreed that Le Testu could join and receive half the treasure.

Drake and Le Testu took twenty French sailors, fifteen English sailors, and a group of Cimaroons and rowed up a river near Nombre de Dios. When they landed, Drake gave strict instructions for the boats to come back for them in four days. They camped so close to Nombre de Dios that the men could hear

Drawing of Drake's knife

carpenters who were working in the harbor at night to escape the heat of the day. Toward morning they heard the bells of mule trains.

Three caravans, one of fifty mules and two of seventy mules each, came toward them. They carried gold and jewels and thirty tons of silver. The mule trains had forty-five soldiers to guard them, "which caused some exchange of bullets and arrows for a time." In the battle, Captain Le Testu was badly wounded and one Cimaroon was killed. The Spanish soldiers fled to seek reinforcements.

Drake's men buried about fifteen tons of silver in the stream and under tree roots. They had barely finished when they heard the Spanish soldiers returning. They retreated to the woods, carrying bars and quoits of gold and boxes of jewels on their shoulders. Captain Le Testu was too badly wounded to keep up, and two of his men volunteered to stay with him while he rested. The others staggered through the woods toward the river for three days, carrying their heavy loads. On the fourth day they saw the river—and seven Spanish pinnaces patrolling it. Their own ships were nowhere to be seen.

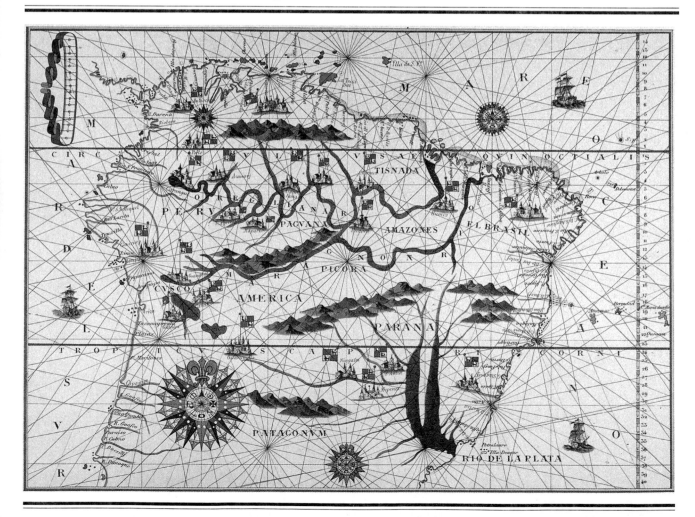

Map of South America, from a Spanish atlas produced in 1582

Drake was sure the Spaniards had found his ships. Each of his men now carried a fortune on his back, and none of it was any use. They were halfway across the world from home, in Spanish territory, with no way of escape.

Drake refused to give in to despair. He exhorted them: "it was no time now to fear; but rather to haste to prevent that which was feared: if the enemy have prevailed against our pinnaces, which God forbid, yet they must have time to search them, . . . we may get to our ships . . . yet by water. Let us therefore make a raft . . . and put ourselves to sea. I will be one, who will be the other?"

Three men volunteered to ride the raft. Pedro, the Cimaroon chief, wanted to go with Drake but had to be left behind because he could not row. The Cimaroons felt such respect and loyalty toward Drake that they offered to let the crew live with their tribe forever, if it were true that their escape was cut off.

The men lashed branches together, made a sail from a biscuit sack, and shaped an oar from a young tree to use as a rudder. Drake leaped on board. He promised the men staying behind that "if it pleased God, he should put his foot in safety aboard his frigate, he would, God willing, by one means or another get them all aboard, in despite of all the Spaniards in the Indies."

This little raft was one of the strangest vessels Drake ever captained. They sailed for nine miles (fourteen kilometers). Most of that time the raft was underwater, submerged by the weight of four men. They were in water up to their waists. Every wave soaked them to the armpits. For six hours the tropical sun beat down on them.

"At length God gave them the sight of two pinnaces." But the pinnaces did not see the little raft. They turned and anchored for the night behind a point of land.

It is amazing that, after all these ordeals, Drake had the energy to play a prank. He put his raft ashore and ran by land around the point. The crew of the pinnaces, seeing him appear so suddenly, thought the Spaniards were chasing him. They took the three men from the raft aboard and asked what had happened to the rest of the company. When Drake answered coldly, "Well . . .," they all thought the expedition had been a failure.

Then Drake grinned and pulled out a quoit of gold and told them the "voyage was made," that everything had been a success.

By dawn Drake had collected the rest of his company, plus the treasure. Captain Le Testu's men were afraid Drake might not give them their share because their captain was not present to protect their interests. Drake told them not to worry. Dividing the gold and silver into two equal portions by weight, he kept half for the English and gave half to the French.

A rescue party searched for Captain Le Testu and his two companions, but they only found one of the Frenchmen. The Spaniards had captured the other two, who revealed the hiding place of all the silver. The earth was dug up in every direction for a mile.

It didn't look as if anything could have been left, but Drake's crew started digging anyway. After three days they had found thirteen bars of silver and some quoits of gold.

Drake asked Pedro and the other Cimaroon chiefs to choose anything they liked as a gift. What Pedro wanted more than anything was the scimitar that Captain Le Tetsu had given to Drake. In return, he offered four quoits of gold that he had hidden. Drake accepted the gold quoits, but instead of keeping them for himself, he added them to the treasure to be divided among the whole crew.

Successful at last, filled with Spanish treasure, Drake's ships turned home to England, arriving in August 1573.

Ships sailing through the English Channel

Chapter 6
The Trial of Thomas Doughty

Queen Elizabeth was delighted with Drake's exploits and with the glorious treasure. The only problem was that she couldn't say so in public, because England was now on friendly terms with Spain. Instead of being a hero at court, Drake disappeared. For three years he served the queen quietly in Ireland. Although Drake never had any children of his own, at this time he became responsible for a young kinsman, John Drake, who was about ten years old. He took the boy with him.

While he was in Ireland, Drake made one of his rare bad judgments about people. He became close friends with Thomas Doughty, a gentleman who had many friends at court. Drake was a self-made man who had grown up poor. He was very bright, but he had little formal education and had taught himself. He was impressed by fine speech, good clothes, money, and titles. Doughty was well educated, wore fancy clothes, and was very charming.

Sir Francis Walsingham

William Cecil, Lord Burghley

Drake dreamed of breaking the Spanish monopoly of the Pacific, raiding the undefended colonies along the western coast of South America, and perhaps even founding English colonies in the New World. He confided these dreams to his wonderful new friend. When they came back from Ireland, Doughty offered to use his influence at court to get backing for the voyage. Doughty was secretary to Sir Christopher Hatton, the Captain of the Guard, who was close to the queen.

Meanwhile, relations between England and Spain had deteriorated again. Many powerful people at court believed war was inevitable. Queen Elizabeth's secretary of state, Sir Francis Walsingham, wanted the war to come soon, while Spain had soldiers and resources tied up quelling a rebellion in the Netherlands. The Lord High Treasurer—William Cecil, Lord Burghley—wanted to postpone war until England was stronger. Queen Elizabeth wanted to weaken Spain without a regular war. She knew that if the treasure ships from Peru did not get to Spain, King Philip would not be able to pay his armies.

Secretary of State Walsingham asked Drake for his ideas. Drake was willing to talk about his plans, but would not put them in writing for good reason. He explained that "her Majesty was mortal, and that if it should please God to take her Majesty away, it might be that some prince might reign that might be in league with the king of Spain, and then will mine own hand be a witness against myself."

Drake was called to the palace to see the queen privately. She wanted to "be revenged on the king of Spain for divers injuries that I have received." She would personally invest in the voyage. But, she said, on no account should Lord Burghley hear of it.

Several high-ranking government officials invested in the enterprise, including Walsingham and Hatton. John Hawkins, who was soon to become treasurer of the navy, also invested. Drake's instructions were, first, to sail through the Strait of Magellan at the southern tip of South America. Since the document bearing his orders is partially destroyed, it is not clear where he was to go after that. It seems he was to explore South America's west coast, or any lands south of South America, or both.

Explorers and mapmakers believed there was an unknown continent in the southern hemisphere to balance the land mass in the northern hemisphere. If he found this continent, Drake was to claim it for England, seek out markets for English goods, and prospect for treasure and rich commodities.

Drake put together a fleet of five ships. He himself commanded the *Pelican*. Drake was now a wealthy man who liked elegance. His flagship had fine oak furniture. The table was set with vessels of pure silver. There were four musicians to entertain at dinner. Drake brought his own drum aboard so he could join in the music.

Young John Drake served as Drake's page and also as ship's artist. Every expedition had a painter whose task was to record the coast accurately. Drake's younger brother, Thomas Drake, was in the crew, as was Diego, his faithful Cimaroon friend.

John Winter was second in command. His ship, the *Elizabeth*, was new and very fine. Winter had two relatives on the Navy Board who were backing the voyage from their own private incomes. John Thomas commanded the thirty-ton *Marigold*, provided by Sir Christopher Hatton.

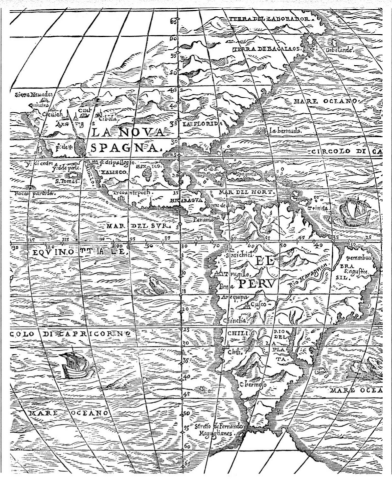

A 1556 map of North and South America, showing the Strait of Magellan at the tip of South America

Thomas Moone commanded one of Drake's pretty little pinnaces, the *Christopher*. He was the ship's carpenter who had drilled holes in the *Swan* back at Nombre de Dios. John Chester commanded the fleet's supply ship, also named the *Swan*. Not many people knew that the supplies stowed aboard included the parts for four more pinnaces.

The crew consisted of 164 sailors, all older and more experienced than those Drake had taken to Nombre de Dios. Missing from the expedition was John Oxenham, who had climbed the tree with Drake to see the Pacific. He had sailed for South America two years before and had not been heard from since. Besides the mariners, the crew included a group of

Portrait of Francis Drake

gentlemen adventurers who paid for the privilege of going on the voyage. They had no training as sailors and did not expect to do any work. They went along for the thrills. Among them was Drake's new friend, Thomas Doughty.

On December 13, 1577, the fleet sailed out of Plymouth harbor. Drake's cover story was that he was going to Alexandria, Egypt, to buy spices. He headed for the Mediterranean, but instead of turning east into the Mediterranean at Gibraltar, he continued south along the coast of Africa. On Christmas Day he set up a temporary base on an island off Morocco. Drake started calling himself "the General," meaning the admiral, and expected the men to use his new title.

As soon as they landed, a party of Moors appeared and offered to trade. The next day a caravan of thirty camels arrived, and "the General" let his men take a small boat to go ashore and bargain. One man, John Fry, was so eager to be first that he jumped out of the boat before it was grounded. He was immediately captured and carried off by the caravan. Drake sent a rescue party, but it was hopeless. Finally on December 31 the fleet moved on. They should have waited a few more days.

The Moors were involved in a civil war and thought Drake's party came from Portugal, which was supporting one side of the war. They captured Fry to interrogate him. When they realized their mistake, they brought him back loaded with gifts. When they

Moors, or Muslims, occupied much of Spain and North Africa from the 600s through the 1400s. This is the Moors' mosque in Cordoba, Spain, built around the year 692.

found Drake's ship had left, they sent him home to England in an English merchant ship. Fry's report was the last firsthand information that anyone had on Drake for a long time.

Drake headed southwest to the Cape Verde Islands, a Portuguese colony in the middle of the Atlantic Ocean. This was the last possible place to get fresh water for the ocean crossing. But the towns had been attacked by pirates. They were deserted and the wells stopped up. There were many streams of fresh water, but the coast was so steep that the shallowest spot was 700 feet (213 meters) deep, and they could not anchor the ships to collect the water.

Outside the capital, Drake captured a Portuguese ship. It had a cargo of fine wine, but it carried an even greater treasure in its Portuguese pilot, Nuño da Silva. Nuño da Silva was a small, dark-bearded man in his fifties. He had crossed the Atlantic many times—as seaman, pilot, navigator, and captain. His expertise was worth more than gold.

Drake renamed the captured ship the *Mary* and added it to his fleet. He gave the Portuguese crew one of the pinnaces in exchange, but he kept the pilot. For the next fifteen months, Nuño da Silva was an unwilling passenger on Drake's voyage. Much of what we know about the voyage comes from his careful records. He reported that Drake brought three navigation books and a map bought in Lisbon. Every time Drake took a ship, he looked at its charts and maps and took any that gave him new information.

Drake made Thomas Doughty captain of the *Mary*. Doughty's new English crew included Drake's younger brother, Thomas, and John Brewer, the trumpeter of the *Pelican*.

Doughty thought that his social status and his financial stake in the voyage entitled him to be Drake's equal in command, although he had no training to be a captain or even a common sailor. Even before the fleet started its long voyage across the ocean, the crew had begun to split into factions for and against Doughty.

There was trouble immediately over a case of petty stealing. John Brewer, the trumpeter, and Ned Bright, a ship's carpenter, accused Captain Thomas Doughty of stealing "some things of great value" and thought he should not "be put in trust any longer." Doughty said Drake's brother Thomas was the thief. Drake found that one of the prisoners had given Doughty some gloves, a ring, and a few coins, "not purloined, but openly given him, and received in the sight of all men." Although the items were trivial, the charge was serious. Drake's strict rule was that all booty was placed in a common pot to be shared. No one, not even the commander, was to take treasure for himself.

Drake made Doughty temporary captain of the flagship *Pelican*, where the gentleman adventurers were. He promoted his brother Thomas Drake to captain of the *Mary*. Then Francis Drake took up temporary residence on the captured ship, along with his brother and Nuño da Silva.

Now the fleet began its voyage across the Atlantic—sixty-three days without sight of land. Chaplain Fletcher thought they were the most privileged of men. While England was in the dark and cold of winter, they were warm and dry and were surrounded by food. Brief thunderstorms supplied drinking water. Even the pesky lice were gone now that the men could wash and change clothes and clean the ship.

Doughty was involved in a second incident with John Brewer. As the ships drifted becalmed along the equator, Brewer rowed over to the *Pelican* to visit his old buddies. Some of the crew decided to play a practical joke called cobbeying. They pulled his pants down and gave him a beating. Doughty either took part or encouraged it. Drake found out and sent Doughty to the *Swan*, the little supply ship where John Chester was captain.

Doughty was furious. Trouble continued between Drake and Doughty throughout the voyage.

Doughty told people that it was through his influence at court that they had gotten backing for the voyage and that he was of equal rank in it to Drake. He hinted that he knew "certain secrets about Francis Drake that he would never divulge, but if he did divulge them, Drake would be both sorry and ashamed."

A ship becalmed in the Sargasso Sea, a thicket of algae near the equator. Calm regions in the ocean were sometimes called the "horse latitudes." That's because crews would throw horses overboard to lighten a ship's load, hoping that the ship would then sail on.

Map of the coast of Brazil, from an early print

Doughty boasted that he possessed supernatural powers and could conjure up the devil. This was not idle talk in the sixteenth century. Most people believed in the devil and sorcery. As a man of his times, Drake probably believed in supernatural powers, too. When they came to the coast of Brazil in April, they began to have incredibly bad weather. Drake may well have wondered if Doughty had power over wind and fog.

The day after they sighted Brazil, they were caught in such a bad storm that none of the ships could see each other. The *Christopher* disappeared for more than a week. Two weeks later, the *Swan* disappeared with Doughty on board. The *Christopher* disappeared again.

On May 10, 1578, Drake took a small boat and went to explore a rocky bay. He was caught in a fog so dense that the ships could not see him. A storm blew up. John Chester took a great risk coming to the rescue in the *Marigold*.

Just before the storm broke, the *Christopher* had reappeared. But after the storm the *Mary* was gone. The *Mary* and the *Swan* were both storeships and carried most of the supplies, including the water. Drake could not winter without them.

As the ships continued to play hide-and-seek in the fog and the storms for days and weeks at a time, Drake decided he had too many ships to keep track of. He determined to reduce the fleet. When the *Swan* was found, it was broken up for firewood. Once again Thomas Doughty changed ships, this time to the flagship *Pelican*.

A storm-wrecked ship

Mount Sarmiento, the highest point of Tierra del Fuego, at the tip of South America

Doughty also tried to bribe some of the sailors. He offered to loan a ship's gunner forty pounds, which was equal to almost a year's pay. Captain John Chester reported that Doughty said if Chester would accept his orders, Doughty would make the ship's company ready to cut one another's throats. In other words, Doughty would cause a mutiny against Drake and put himself in charge.

Drake brought his fleet into Port St. Julian, just 200 miles (322 kilometers) north of the Strait of Magellan. In this place fifty-eight years earlier, Magellan had hanged the officers responsible for a mutiny on his expedition. Drake's men found the remains of the gallows and the bones of the hanged men

Engraving of Francis Drake, copied from an original painting

at its base. Their ship's cooper used the gallows wood to make drinking tankards.

In this desolate winter place at the edge of the world, Drake charged Thomas Doughty with mutiny and attempting the "overthrow of this voyage." Drake was the judge. He named forty men to the jury, including Doughty's friends and supporters. The trial proceeded quietly until Doughty let fall that he had given Lord Burghley a plan of the voyage. Drake was enraged. Doughty had betrayed the secret purpose of the expedition to the one man the queen had said must not be told. The jury brought in a verdict of guilty. Drake asked for the death sentence and no one opposed him.

Doughty died with more grace than he had lived. He and Drake knelt together for communion. They had dinner together, drank a farewell toast, and acted like old friends. At the block, Doughty joked with the executioner and prayed for the queen and the happy outcome of the voyage. When the ax had fallen, Drake ordered the head to be held up and formally called out, "Lo, there is the end to traitors."

A month after the trial and execution, Drake assembled his men ashore and ordered everyone to make confession to the chaplain and take communion. When Chaplain Fletcher offered to give a sermon, Drake said, "Nay, soft, Master Fletcher, I must preach this day myself." Francis Drake gave a sermon that is still the basis for the rules that govern people at sea.

In his sermon, Drake reminded the company of the dangers they were about to face. "We must have these mutinies and discords that are grown among us redressed. . . . Here is such controversy between the sailors and the gentlemen . . . that it doth even make me mad to hear it." He demanded that sailors and gentlemen work together, a revolutionary concept. "For I must have the gentleman to haul and draw with the mariner and the mariner with the gentleman."

If anyone did not want to sail with him under these rules, Drake said, they could take the *Marigold* and find their way back to England. "But let them take heed that they go straight homeward, for if I find them in my way I will surely sink them."

When every man agreed to follow him, Drake turned to his captains and relieved them of their commands, making the point that he had absolute authority. He spoke for the last time about the execution of Doughty. He told them that others in the company deserved the same fate, but they had all taken confession, and "as I am a gentleman, there shall no more die."

He told the entire crew how the venture had come about and who the backers were, including the queen herself. Then he reinstated the ship's officers.

Drake reduced his fleet to three ships, the *Elizabeth*, the *Marigold*, and the *Pelican*. He renamed the *Pelican* the *Golden Hind*, after the symbol of a hind, or deer, on Sir Christopher Hatton's coat of arms. This was a good political move. Hatton had been Doughty's employer, and he was a favorite at court.

Finally, on August 17, 1578, Drake set sail from Port St. Julian. On August 20, he led his three ships into the Strait of Magellan.

The Golden Hind

Chapter 7
The World Encompassed

The Strait of Magellan was 300 miles (483 kilometers) of strong currents, sharp rocks, furious winds, and tides that could rise forty feet (twelve meters). The great Magellan took thirty-seven days to get through it. Drake and his men had incredibly good luck with the weather and made it through in sixteen days. They caught two thousand large, flightless birds that looked like geese. The Welsh sailors called them whiteheads or "pen gwynns." They cut down a tree so big it took two men's arms to encircle the trunk. Drake wanted it as a present for Queen Elizabeth. They put it in the hold for ballast.

Three days after they emerged into the Pacific Ocean, Balboa's great South Sea, a storm blew without ceasing for three weeks. Winds blew with hurricane strength. An eclipse of the moon seemed to be an omen that God was against them. Captain John Thomas's little *Marigold* sank with all hands. Ned Bright was one of the twenty-nine sailors on board. Chaplain Fletcher was on watch on the *Golden Hind* and thought he heard the cries of the drowning sailors in the "mountains of the sea." John Brewer, Drake's trumpeter, was knocked overboard by a stray rope and narrowly escaped drowning.

The *Elizabeth* and the *Golden Hind* were blown 300 miles (483 kilometers) south of the Strait of Magellan. Then Drake saw for himself that there was no unknown southern continent. The Atlantic and Pacific oceans "met in a most large and free scope." Geographically speaking, this was the most important discovery of the voyage.

On October 8, the two remaining ships dropped anchor in a sheltered spot. But the *Golden Hind* lost its anchor. In the darkness the ships lost sight of each other. John Winter, the captain of the *Elizabeth*, waited several days for Drake, lighting fires to show his position. Winter could not convince his men to continue the voyage. The *Elizabeth* returned to England. The investors and the queen were not pleased. John Winter served a term in prison and his career was ruined.

The *Golden Hind* was blown far south and battered for weeks by storms. After a year at sea, Drake had only one ship left. Of the 164 men who left Plymouth, only eighty were still with him. But the wild storm finally died, and it was time to sail the South Sea and explore the western coast of South America.

The *Golden Hind* anchored at an island off the coast of present-day Chile. Drake went ashore with a group of men. The local Indians seemed friendly, but when Drake and his crew of eleven came back the next day for water, they were ambushed by a hundred Indians. Every man was hit. Drake had three arrow wounds, one just under his right eye. Diego, his faithful Cimaroon friend who had been with him since Nombre de Dios six years before, had twenty wounds. John Brewer had seventeen. They had no doctor, for the surgeon had died. Most of the men recovered, but Diego died.

Magellanic penguins, named for the famous explorer, in southern Chile

Two weeks later, Drake sailed into a harbor at Valparaíso, Chile. The crew of a Spanish ship invited the newcomers over for wine. They did not dream that a ship coming in from the Pacific Ocean could be anything but Spanish. Thomas Moone rowed over with a boarding party. One Spaniard jumped overboard and warned the villagers, who fled into the hills. Drake took possession of the village. His men found wine and provisions in the warehouses.

The Spaniards had no quick way to warn the other cities. Drake continued north, poking into undefended harbors and river mouths. One day they surprised a Spaniard asleep on a hillside beside his mules. He was coming back from the mines, and his mules carried thirteen bars of silver. Later they came upon another Spaniard with a train of eight llamas, each carrying a hundred pounds of silver.

Drake continued north taking small prizes. His destination was Callao, the port that served Lima, Peru. Lima was the most important city in the Spanish empire of South America. He had been told that a treasure ship had just arrived there. Callao harbor was crowded with ships. At 10:00 at night, the *Golden Hind* slipped in unnoticed. Drake learned that the treasure ship had already been unloaded.

He got the first news from Europe in over a year. The kings of Morocco, Portugal, and the Moorish kingdom of Fez had been killed in battle on the same day. The pope and the king of France had died. He also learned that twenty-six Protestant prisoners had recently been burned at the stake in Lima. Among the prisoners in dungeons in Lima was his friend, John Oxenham, who had stood with him in the tree when he first saw the Pacific Ocean.

CALIOV DE LIMA

The harbor of Callao, Peru, from an illustration published in 1620

About this time, the authorities realized there was a strange ship in the harbor and came to check. Drake decided it was time to leave Callao. First, he cut the cables of every ship in the harbor and chopped down the masts of the bigger ships so he could not be pursued. When young John Drake fell into the hands of the Inquisition on a later expedition, he explained that Drake hoped to capture the drifting ships afterwards and use them to bargain for the lives of Oxenham and the other English captives. Drake also wrote a letter to the viceroy of Peru warning him not to execute Oxenham or any other English prisoner. But Oxenham was hanged the following year.

The governor of Callao had sent an urgent dispatch to the viceroy in Lima. The viceroy distributed weapons, and two ships were found in condition to sail.

They gave chase for most of the night, but Drake had too much of a lead. The viceroy was so furious that he sentenced the ships' officers to exile and heavy fines.

Actually, Drake had a narrow escape. He was barely out of sight of Callao when he ran into a dead calm. They were close enough to town for the crew to hear the bells ringing the alarm.

While he was at Callao, Drake had heard of a great treasure ship that had just sailed for Panama. It was nicknamed the *Cacafuego*, politely translated as the *Spitfire*. For two weeks he chased his elusive prey. He promised a gold chain to the man who first sighted it. Along the way he captured four other prizes. One ship had a large crucifix and emeralds as long as a man's finger. The emeralds eventually decorated Queen Elizabeth's crown.

Offshore islands in the Pacific off Lima, Peru

On March 1, young John Drake called down from the masthead that he could see the *Cacafuego*'s sails on the horizon. The treasure ship was not well armed, and the captain had no suspicion of an enemy. The *Golden Hind* was almost alongside the *Cacafuego* when he heard Francis Drake call to him, "Strike sail, Señor Juan de Anton, unless you wish to go to the bottom."

The treasure in this one ship made good all the losses that Drake and Hawkins and others had suffered over the years. Eighty pounds of bar gold, thirteen chests of pieces of eight, jewels, pearls, and twenty-six tons of silver! One sailor watching the flow

Drake and his men unloading treasure from the Cacafuego

of silver pouring into the *Golden Hind* suggested that the *Cacafuego* should change its name from *Spitfire* to *Spitsilver*.

It was time for the *Golden Hind* to disappear. All of South America would be on guard against Drake. He returned the *Cacafuego* to its captain. Drake said he was returning to England and that he had four possible routes. Shortly after leaving the *Cacafuego*, Drake captured a small ship. On board were two pilots who had with them all the charts and sailing directions for crossing the Pacific. Drake may have planned to circumnavigate the world all along. Or, he may have decided on the route after these charts fell into his hands.

On April 4, 1579, Drake captured a Spanish merchant ship laden with silks and porcelain from China. Its captain, Don Francisco de Zarate, wrote a report to the viceroy of Mexico. This viceroy was Don Martin Enriquez, the same man who had treated Hawkins and Drake with such treachery at San Juan de Ulúa.

"This Drake," Zarate wrote, "is a cousin of John Hawkins, and the same man that sacked Nombre de Dios five years ago. He seems to be about thirty-five years old and has a reddish beard. . . . He treats all of his men with affection and they treat him with respect . . . he calls [his council] together and listens to what they have to say before giving his order—although, in fact, he pays no real attention to anyone."

Zarate noted how disciplined the sailors were. "When they came to capture our ship, not a single one of them dared take anything without his orders." He paid tribute to Francis and John Drake's skill as artists, "painters, who depict the coastline in all its true colors. This was something that troubled me a great deal, for whoever follows him can easily find his way."

Before he left Spanish waters, Drake released the Portuguese pilot Nuño da Silva and put him aboard a ship bound for Panama. Da Silva did not fare well. While he had been Drake's prisoner, Portugal had come under Spain's control. The viceroy of Mexico handed him over to the Inquisition, and he was tortured and imprisoned for three years. He was then sent to Spain and imprisoned in Seville. Fortunately, King Philip became curious about a man who had actually known the pirate Drake, and he ordered him to be released.

Drake continued up the west coast of North America as far north as Vancouver, Canada, where he encountered "most vile, thick and stinking fogs." Off the California coast, he reported that the rigging grew solid with ice and that meat froze soon after being taken from the oven. This seems unlikely in California in June. Drake must have had very unusual weather, or his usually accurate measurements were wrong. Or, he may have deliberately put in false material to make the area sound worthless so others would not explore there.

The *Golden Hind* was straining and leaking from the weight of the silver in the hold. Drake needed a harbor for cleaning and repairs. He anchored in a small bay just north of San Francisco. The bay just east of Point Reyes is the most likely place. It is called Drake's Bay.

The local Indians flocked down to see the strange white men. They honored Drake and his crew with presents and ceremonies. The chief set a feathered headdress on Drake's head. Chaplain Fletcher thought they were asking Drake to become their king. More likely they were making him an honorary chief. Drake

Sea lions and rocks at Drake's Bay, Point Reyes National Seashore, California

Indians of California, Drake's New Albion, honoring him as a chief

stayed a month and called the country New Albion, claiming it for England. When the *Golden Hind* sailed, the Indians "took a sorrowful farewell of us . . . they presently ran to the top of the hills to keep us in sight as long as they could."

It took three months to make the long Pacific crossing to the Moluccas, or Spice Islands. Portugal controlled the Spice Islands but had earned the hatred of a local ruler, the sultan of Ternate. Drake was royally received by the sultan. Giant war canoes towed the *Golden Hind* into the harbor. Drake responded by having the ship's musicians play. The sultan was so pleased he asked for the musicians to be put into a small boat so he could tow them behind his canoe. When the *Golden Hind* set sail again, in addition to the treasure from the *Cacafuego*, it carried six tons of cloves worth their weight in gold.

Between the Moluccas and the Indian Ocean was a region of uncharted islands, rocks, and swift currents. On the evening of January 9, 1580, the ship struck a submerged reef. The men knew it might be only minutes before the ship broke up and they were all at the bottom of the sea. Drake told his men to kneel and pray. Chaplain Fletcher apparently gave an "all is lost" type of sermon.

Drake checked the damage. Surprisingly, the reef had not torn a hole in the ship. The *Golden Hind* was built with a special double lining invented by John Hawkins, which may have given extra protection. But on one side of the reef the water was only one fathom deep and the ship needed more than two fathoms. The other side was so deep they could not put an anchor down. That meant they couldn't attach a cable and pull the ship off the reef. Sooner or later wind and waves would break the ship.

All night the crew worked to free the ship, but to no avail. The prevailing wind drove them farther on to the reef. At morning prayers, Chaplain Fletcher gave everyone communion. Drake told them to be of good cheer. They had done what they could for their souls; now they should do what they could to look after their bodies. Drake jettisoned eight guns. Three tons of cloves went overboard. If the giant tree trunk from the Strait of Magellan was still in the hold, it probably went overboard too. Drake even sacrificed a great quantity of provisions, "enough to break the heart of a miser to think on it," said one sailor. The one thing he didn't give up was the treasure.

At 4:00 P.M. the ship began to heel toward the deep water. The men thought their final moment had come. Then, like a miracle, the wind shifted direction. The men hoisted the sail and the *Golden Hind* righted itself and floated safely into the deep water.

They continued to navigate through the labyrinth of rocks and reefs of Southeast Asian waters. They traveled across the Indian Ocean and around the Cape of Good Hope, Africa's southern tip. The Portuguese had called the cape "the most dangerous cape in the world, never without intolerable storms." Drake proved the information was false.

On September 26, 1580, two years and ten months after the journey began, Drake's men sighted Plymouth Sound.

Sir Francis Drake

Chapter 8
A War with Spain Is Coming

Before he entered Plymouth harbor, Drake hailed some fishermen and asked a vital question.

"Is the queen alive and well?"

The answer came, "Her Majesty is in good health, but there is pestilence in Plymouth."

Drake anchored behind St. Nicholas Island, the same island where his family had sought refuge when he was eight years old. Drake's wife, Mary, and the mayor of Plymouth rowed out to the ship and gave him the latest news.

A Protestant revolt against Spanish rule in the Low Countries—modern Belgium, The Netherlands, and Luxembourg—had begun to fall apart. The Catholic nobles in Belgium had returned to Spanish control. King Philip's nephew, the Duke of Parma, was commanding the forces against the rebel Protestant provinces.

With the king of Portugal dead, Philip of Spain was about to take over Portugal and all its possessions in Africa, the Pacific, and Brazil. He would also own the Portuguese fleet of armed galleons. All the lands the pope had divided with the Line of Demarcation would be united. Philip would be the most powerful ruler in the world. There were reports that Spain was building an immense fleet of ships to use first against the Netherlands and then against England.

In the midst of these political shifts, Drake had arrived with a ship loaded with Spanish treasure. The first thing he did was to get the treasure off the ship and safely under guard at Plymouth Castle. He heard from friends at court that some of the queen's most experienced advisors, including Lord Burghley, thought the plunder should be restored to Spain.

Drake received orders from the queen to come to court without delay and bring samples of the interesting objects he had found on his travels. He went to London with a pack train of horses loaded with silver, gold, and jewels. The queen talked with him in secret for six hours. The treasure was to be registered and stored in the Tower of London until a way could be found to restore it to its rightful owners. That way was never found, and the treasure stayed in England.

On New Year's Day, 1581, Queen Elizabeth wore a new emerald crown at court. In April 1581, the queen went down in state to visit the *Golden Hind*. Drake knelt before her on the deck and was knighted.

Sir Francis Drake lived on land for the next few years. In 1581 he was made mayor of Plymouth. He bought Buckland Abbey, a former monastery that had been converted into a great country estate. It was just six miles (ten kilometers) from the humble farm cottage where he had been born. Two oil paintings of Drake and a legendary drum that he took with him around the world can be seen today at Buckland Abbey.

In 1583, Drake's wife, Mary, died. In 1584 he began a term in the House of Commons, the lower house of the English Parliament. The following year, he married Elizabeth Sydenham. He traveled constantly to London, working with Walsingham and John Hawkins, preparing England for the coming war with Spain.

Queen Elizabeth I of England, who liked wearing a lot of jewels

Queen Elizabeth knighting Drake aboard the Golden Hind

Lord Burghley had appointed John Hawkins treasurer of the navy in 1577. Hawkins was a businessman and a seaman and he was honest. He had commanded ocean expeditions and knew what was needed to keep a fighting fleet able to stay at sea for months at a time. Hawkins remembered the *Jesus of Lübeck*, the floating-castle-style ship he had to abandon at San Juan de Ulúa. Once he was on the Navy Board, Hawkins designed new ships of war that were low-built, moderate in size, and seaworthy. When older ships came into drydock for repairs, he had them rebuilt so drastically that they were almost new ships. They were faster, sailed closer into the wind, and had less need of repairs. In his first five years, he converted the old fleet into a modern navy.

Hawkins also reformed the way the fleet was manned and how the men were paid. In the old navy, as many men as possible were crowded into the ships, even though hand-to-hand combat was no longer the most important part of fighting. Hawkins said that overcrowding caused unclean conditions that led to epidemics. It also tied the ships to their home ports because they constantly needed food supplies. He pointed out that low pay meant that only the "rag and tag" would remain in the navy. He gave figures to show that a lower number of well paid men would not cost any more and would give better service. Lord Burghley was convinced and raised the pay scale.

The Spanish ambassador, Bernardino de Mendoza, reported home to Spain: "They are building ships endlessly, and are thus making themselves masters of the sea. Seeing their country with such multitudes of ships helps to swell their pride, and they think that there is no prince on earth who can come against them."

In 1585, conditions between Spain and England took a drastic turn. Spain faced a famine because its grain crop failed. Spain was England's best customer, and many English ships carried grain to Spain. While they were in the Spanish harbors, the ships were seized, the cargoes confiscated, and the crews thrown in jail.

One English ship escaped. The *Primrose* was discharging its cargo at Biscay, on the north coast of Spain. All of a sudden, a party of soldiers disguised as merchants came on board with the corregidor, or sheriff, of Biscay. They demanded that the ship surrender. But the crew threw the Spaniards into the water and made for England with the corregidor still on board. In his pocket was Philip II's authorization to seize the English ships.

Philip II of Spain

Martin Frobisher, an explorer in his own right

Sir Francis Drake was chosen to teach the Spanish king a lesson. He was to strike the hardest blow he could at the colonies that provided Spain with wealth. Drake called it "singeing the king of Spain's beard."

Drake led a force of twenty-nine ships. It was a private force, but the queen contributed two ships from the navy. The vice admiral was Martin Frobisher. Frobisher had made several voyages to the New World, but he had not brought back treasure. Drake's brother Thomas Drake was one of the captains. So was Thomas Moone, the former carpenter. Christopher Carleill, Secretary of State Walsingham's son-in-law, was in charge of land forces. Carleill was a good soldier who had learned his craft helping the Dutch fight Spain.

St. Vincent, one of the Cape Verde Islands in the Atlantic Ocean

Drake sailed immediately to Vigo in northwestern Spain. He used a Spanish port to make his preparations for the Atlantic voyage, and he did it deliberately to insult the king. All of Europe soon heard about his exploits.

Next Drake sacked and burned towns on the Cape Verde Islands, which had belonged to Portugal and now belonged to Spain. It was a bad decision. The islanders had a fever, and the crews caught the infection.

On New Year's Day, 1586, Drake attacked the wealthy and beautiful city of San Domingo in the West Indies. He had learned from a local pilot that the entrance to the harbor was well fortified, but there was an excellent landing place only ten miles (sixteen kilometers) from the city. Drake bombarded the castle, while his little boats and pinnaces moved back and

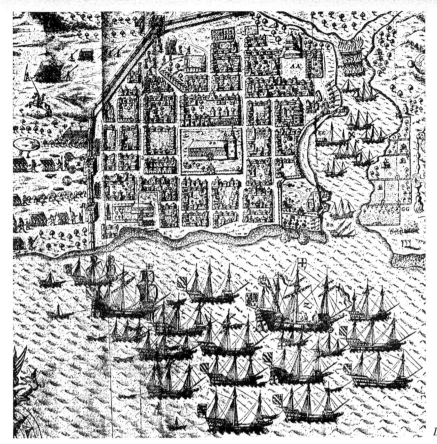

Drake's attack on San Domingo

forth looking as if they were getting ready to ferry a landing force ashore.

In the meantime, Christopher Carleill had landed his soldiers and marched ten miles to join Drake. The Spaniards were totally surprised, and the city fell. One of Drake's first acts was to free the galley slaves in the ships and the African slaves in the city. He gave them arms so they could fight too.

During the negotiations to ransom the city, a Spanish officer raised a flag of truce. Drake sent a black servant to him with a message. The Spanish officer considered this an insult and killed the messenger. Drake immediately hanged two Spanish friars and sent word that he would hang prisoners every day until the officer was executed. This is the only time that Drake is known to have killed a prisoner.

Castillo San Marcos at St. Augustine, Florida, Spain's first colony in what is now the United States

Drake used similar surprise tactics on Cartagena, the great city on the Spanish Main. The harbor lay in a great lagoon protected from the open sea by a low-lying peninsula. The fleet entered the lagoon. While Frobisher made a fake attack, Carleill marched his soldiers down the peninsula.

Drake demolished the Spanish defenses and carried off their guns. His troops, however, were dropping with the tropical fever they had caught in the Cape Verde Islands. He had already lost a third of his men. Captain Thomas Moone was one of the casualties. Drake accepted a ransom for Cartagena and cancelled a plan to attack Panama.

Next, Drake moved up the coast of North America and burned the Spanish settlement of St. Augustine in Florida. Continuing up the coast, he reached the struggling little English colony of Roanoke and offered to leave a ship and a month's rations. The colonists decided instead to abandon the colony, and Drake brought them home to England.

The voyage was not a financial success. Drake had taken no Spanish treasure fleets and captured no treasure trains. But he had made King Philip look foolish in the eyes of the world, and he had cost Spain a tremendous amount of money. The Bank of Spain broke. The Bank of Venice nearly went under. The great German bank of Augsburg refused to extend Philip any more credit.

By 1586, it was known that Philip was preparing to invade England. His admiral, the Marqués de Santa Cruz, drew up a plan for sending a great fleet and an army directly from Spain to southern England. It was too expensive. Philip was bankrupt except for the treasure fleets.

Replica of the Golden Hind *moored at St. Augustine*

The plan was changed. The fleet would sail from Spain up the English Channel and pick up the Duke of Parma's army that was serving in the Netherlands. Philip began building ships. Guns were a problem, though. Spain did not make big guns and had to buy them from Italy. Drake had captured 240 of them in his raids.

Cliffs of Cape St. Vincent near Sagres, Portugal

English spies reported that Spain's invasion was planned for the summer of 1587. Queen Elizabeth instructed Drake to stop the gathering of the Spanish fleets and even to attack the ships in the harbors. Then she changed her mind and tried to cancel the orders, but Drake thought this might happen and had left Plymouth early.

He took his fleet immediately to the great Spanish harbor of Cadiz. He told his captains he planned to go in all at once and cause as much damage as he could. His vice admiral, William Borough, objected. Drake ignored him. There were about eighty Spanish ships in the harbor. Drake claimed he destroyed thirty-seven of them, including the brand new galleon belonging to Admiral Santa Cruz. Spain admitted a loss of twenty-four ships.

Next Drake headed for Cape St. Vincent, between Cadiz and Lisbon, Portugal. Jutting out into the sea, this cape was Portugal's southwesternmost point of land. He planned to capture a fortress there so that he would have a landing place. Vice Admiral Borough complained that Drake was not consulting his captains. Drake put him under arrest, took away his command, and made him a prisoner on his own ship, the *Golden Lion*. Drake personally led a landing party at Sagres, on Cape St. Vincent, and helped pile the wood to burn the fortress gates.

Next he sailed north to Lisbon to seek action with Admiral Santa Cruz. Lisbon was too strongly defended, and Drake had to settle for insulting and taunting Santa Cruz. He returned to Cape St. Vincent, where he burned thousands of wooden staves intended to make barrels for storing food and water.

Drake heard that a Spanish carrack was coming from the East Indies. These ships usually carried great fortunes. He headed for the Azores Islands to intercept it. Some of the ships in his fleet were running low on food. The men thought they had done enough and wanted to go home.

The *Golden Lion*, where William Borough was held prisoner, deserted. The men refused to obey the captain and took the ship home. Drake, who had a temper, decided Borough had caused the mutiny. He held a court martial and sentenced Borough to death in his absence. Later, in London, calmer heads overturned Drake's hasty action.

Drake still had enough men to overcome the carrack. Named the *San Felipe*, it proved to be the greatest single prize ever taken in Drake's lifetime, greater even than the *Cacafuego*. Now with something grand to show for his efforts, Drake sailed his prize back to England. The cargo of spices, jewels, silks, and porcelains from China was worth millions. It more than paid for the whole campaign.

Not knowing the English fleet had gone home, King Philip sent Admiral Santa Cruz to the Azores Islands to protect other carracks. Santa Cruz came back to Lisbon in October. Philip wanted his great fleet to sail against England in the autumn of 1587, but Santa Cruz said the ships were not ready. Santa Cruz died of worry and overwork in February 1588.

King Philip chose the Duke of Medina Sidonia to replace Santa Cruz and lead the fleet. Medina Sidonia had handled the Cadiz attack well, protecting the town from further damage. The only problem was that the duke did not want the job of commander. He wrote to King Philip and explained that he was a bad choice. He had no experience in naval warfare and he easily became seasick. But the king insisted, and Medina Sidonia loyally obeyed. He went to Lisbon to finish preparing the fleet. In May 1588, the Invincible Armada was ready to sail.

A ship of the Spanish Armada

Chapter 9
The Armada

In May 1588, the largest fleet of armed ships the world had ever seen assembled in the Portuguese port of Lisbon. It totalled nearly 130 ships and it was nicknamed the Invincible Armada. Its purpose was to bring England under Spanish and Catholic rule.

Common Spaniards in the street recited a little jingle:

> *My brother Don Juan*
> *To England has gone*
> *To kill the Drake*
> *And the Queen to take*
> *And the heretics all to destroy.*

The Duke of Medina Sidonia, commander of the Armada, reminded the crews that they were on a sacred mission. He carried a special banner from the altar of the Cathedral of Lisbon aboard his flagship, the *San Martin*. On May 23, 1588, the great Armada moved out into the Atlantic. It moved slowly because, in order to keep together, the whole fleet had to move at the speed of the slowest ship. Almost immediately, a great storm struck and scattered the ships for miles. Keeping food and water fresh became critical. Many of the storage casks were made of unseasoned green wood that warped. Water leaked out and food spoiled. Sir Francis Drake had burned the supply of seasoned barrels in his raid the year before.

The Armada struggled into the port of Corunna, on Spain's northwest coast, to make repairs and to form itself back into a single unit. Medina Sidonia wrote to King Philip. He explained that sickness was spreading among his men and the ships had been damaged by the weather. He begged the king to postpone the Armada's mission for a year.

King Philip refused. He ordered the Armada to attack England as soon as possible. The loyal duke sighed and obeyed his king. The fleet set out again through fierce storms. The weather was so bad that thirty ships were lost.

The English fleet, under Admiral Charles Howard and Vice Admiral Francis Drake, was having equally bad trouble with the weather. They wanted to meet up with the enemy on the open sea, far from England. When they got near the Spanish coast, gale winds blew them all the way back to Plymouth. But the storm that seemed to be against them was really a blessing. They might have been on the coast of Spain when the Armada attacked England. Admiral Howard wrote, "God blessed us with turning us back."

Howard and Drake were playing a game of lawn bowling when a little bark named after the *Golden Hind* sighted the Armada near the English Channel. Its captain, Thomas Fleming, raced to Plymouth to give them the news. According to tradition, Francis Drake replied, "There is time enough to finish the game and beat the Spaniards too." Drake was right. The wind and the tide were both wrong. Ships could not put out to sea until the tide changed many hours later.

If the Spaniards had sent their fastest ships ahead, they might have pinned the English fleet in Plymouth Sound. Medina Sidonia held a council of war off "the

Lizard," the southwestern tip of England. His vice admiral, Juan Martinez de Recalde, and others urged him to attack, but the duke had specific instructions from King Philip. He was to continue up the English Channel until he linked with the Duke of Parma, who was coming down from the Netherlands. Even while they were discussing their plans, the opportunity passed. Drake and Howard were sailing out of Plymouth Sound.

Twenty-four large fighting ships and forty smaller ships had gotten clear of Plymouth by noon on July 20. Three hours later, the English fleet sighted the Armada. Drake wrote in his first dispatch that he saw "above a hundred sails, many great ships."

The Armada traveled in the pattern of a giant crescent with the tips pointing backwards. The main fighting ships formed the center and the tips of the crescent. Storeships and auxiliaries came behind the main battle line and were protected by two more squadrons of warships. The entire Armada moved with incredible precision.

Spanish ships were huge. They were designed to carry large cargoes across the ocean. English ships were much smaller but more maneuverable because they were designed to work in the shifting winds of

The Armada sailing in its crescent-shaped formation

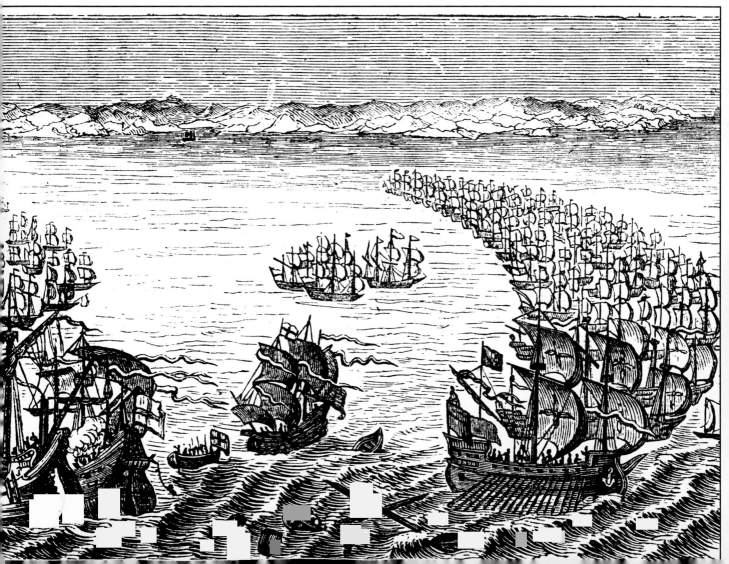

the English Channel and the North Sea. To the English sailors, the Armada seemed to fill the horizon.

At sunset it rained. All night long, the English ships continued to work their way out of Plymouth harbor and along the coast. This was a great feat of seamanship totally unexpected by the Spaniards. It was possible only because John Hawkins had rebuilt the English navy with sleek, modern ships. At daybreak on July 21, Spain had lost its advantage. The English ships had come around to the far side of the Armada, where the wind would benefit them.

*The coast of Devon
on the English Channel*

A new form of warfare was about to take place, but the admirals of the two fleets exchanged courtesies that went back to medieval times. Admiral Howard, on his ship the *Ark Royale*, ordered a shot fired to declare war formally. From the deck of the *San Martin*, the Duke of Medina Sidonia raised the consecrated banner from the Cathedral of Lisbon.

In the old form of warfare, ships powered by oars rammed each other. The new navy crippled or sank the enemy by firing broadsides, or cannon volleys from the sides of the ships. In this kind of fighting, the wind was as important as the ships. On the first day, the wind favored the English. They could attack any ship that separated from the Armada, while the Spanish ships had to sail against the wind. The English concentrated on attacking two ships, trying to cripple them and force them out of the pattern. Vice Admiral Recalde's ship lost a mast. He fought for over an hour before the *San Martin* and the *Rosario* came to the rescue. The *Rosario* collided with another ship and was damaged, although the English didn't know it. Both sides came out of this action with respect for the enemy.

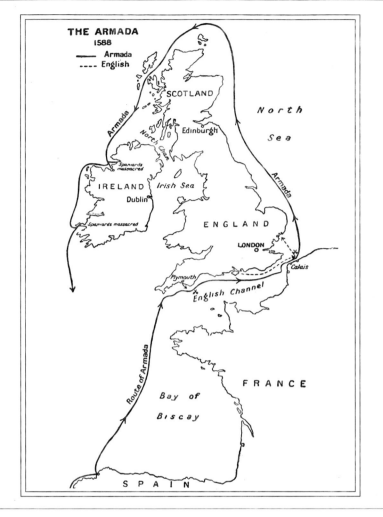

Route of the Spanish Armada from Spain through its retreat around Scotland and Ireland

The first major disaster had nothing to do with the fighting. The *San Salvador*, an 800-ton Spanish galleon, suddenly exploded and the top two decks were blown off. This kind of accident happened often on wooden ships that carried large quantities of gunpowder. In this case, it may have been ignited on purpose by a Dutch gunner in revenge for being forced to fight on the side of his own country's enemy. The *San Salvador* carried the Armada's paymaster and the treasure chests. The entire Armada came almost to a halt while the valuable ship was towed to the center of the crescent where it could be protected.

Admiral Howard fully expected the Spaniards to try and take Plymouth harbor. Naturally, they would have to seize a port in order to land an army. The Spanish officers had the same idea, but Medina Sidonia had his instructions from the king to wait for Parma.

When the fighting ended for the day, Admiral Howard gave orders to follow the Armada through the night to keep it away from shore. Drake led on the *Revenge*. Howard and the rest of the fleet followed him, steering by a lantern on the stern of the *Revenge*. Just before dawn, the lantern went out and Drake disappeared.

In the dark, Admiral Howard continued to follow the light of a ship he thought was the *Revenge*. When dawn came, he discovered the light was on one of the Armada's ships, and that his ship and two others were mixed in with the rear guard of the Armada!

Medina Sidonia could have captured the leader of the English forces, but he didn't know it. He was coping with other problems. The *San Salvador* was sinking. The paymaster, the treasure chests, and the officers and men who were not too badly wounded were taken off. Two galleasses were commanded to sink the ship. But before they could reach it, English ships came to attack. The same Captain Fleming who had brought Drake the first news of the Armada towed the *San Salvador* away. It carried a cargo worth more to England than the treasure chests—fourteen brass cannon, four iron cannon, 132 barrels of powder, and 2,246 cannonballs.

Drake was not part of this battle. He was gone for nearly eighteen hours. When he turned up, he too had captured a Spanish ship. Prize money and the ransom money for captives went to the captors, so this was a great piece of luck. Here is the story he told.

By the light of a quarter moon, Drake saw the sails of ships moving on the seaward side of the Armada. He chased them, but first he extinguished his lantern so the English fleet would not follow him. The ships turned out to be German merchantmen that had accidentally stumbled into the battle zone. Seeing that the German ships were not dangerous, Drake hurried to catch up to the fleet he was supposed to be leading. Suddenly he came upon the *Rosario*, the ship that had been damaged in a collision while helping Vice Admiral Recalde. The *Rosario* was alone and had lost its

The Spanish Armada moving up the English Channel

mainmast. Drake sailed up and shouted for the *Rosario* to surrender, and do it quickly because he was in a hurry.

He was bluffing. The *Rosario* had forty-six guns and over three hundred soldiers. But Drake's name had such power that the ship surrendered. Tradition says the beautiful altar in the parish church in Rye comes from that ship of the Armada.

Admiral Howard accepted Drake's story, but no one else had seen the mysterious German ships. Martin Frobisher, one of the squadron leaders, was jealous because Drake would get the prize money. He accused Drake of being either a coward or a traitor.

For more than three centuries, Drake's story was under suspicion and his reputation tarnished. It was not until 1926 that his story was confirmed. That year, a German ship captain's report from 1588 was discovered. The captain reported coming through the English Channel and being stopped by Sir Francis Drake.

On Tuesday, July 23, the English ships darted in and out, constantly changing patterns to confuse the Armada. Although it looked like a lot of action, very few shots were actually fired because the English were almost out of ammunition. By Wednesday, more supplies had arrived, but the wind was dead calm.

On Thursday, a major battle was fought off the Isle of Wight, near England's southern coast. The wind kept shifting direction, favoring first one side, then the other. At one point the English fleet had the Armada on the run, pushing it against sandbanks so it would go aground. Then the wind changed and the Spanish fleet escaped into deep water and headed for the safety of France. The English fleet could not go in pursuit because it was out of ammunition.

Friday, July 26, was another day of windless calm. Admiral Howard bestowed the honor of knighthood on his squadron leaders John Hawkins and Martin Frobisher.

On Saturday, Medina Sidonia crossed the English Channel and anchored his fleet near Calais, France. Three times he had sent pinnaces to Dunkirk, farther up the coast, begging Parma for forty light ships that could match the English in quick maneuvers. While he waited desperately for reinforcements, an entire squadron of ships arrived to strengthen the English. Medina Sidonia was trapped with the enemy on one

Admiral Howard knighting his captains aboard the Ark Royale

side and miles of sandbanks on the other. Why did he hold to his orders and wait for Parma?

The captured captain of the *Rosario* gave one possible explanation. He said that the Duke of Parma, who was Philip II's nephew, was the commander in chief of the mission. Medina Sidonia's job was to hand over his forces to Parma and act under his orders.

*Alexander Farnese,
Duke of Parma*

Medina Sidonia did not know that Parma could not leave the Netherlands. The commander of the Dutch fleet, Justin of Nassau, had blockaded Dunkirk. A dozen little warships patrolled the ports. Outside Dunkirk were long sandbanks that were a danger to any ship needing more than 5 feet (1.5 meters) of water. The Spanish ships needed at least 25 feet. The Armada could not get in, and Parma could not get out.

The battle with the Armada had been going on for a week. The arrival of the extra squadron meant the English forces were at their maximum strength. It was time for decisive action. Sir Francis Drake volunteered to sacrifice one of his ships as a fireship. Seven others joined him.

Sunday afternoon Drake changed his squadron's position so that it was upwind from the Spanish fleet. A little after midnight when the tide turned, the eight English ships moved toward the Armada under full sail, but without showing a single light. Suddenly the ships blazed with fire. Their crews walked amid the flames, steering straight toward the Spanish fleet until they were so close the Armada could not escape. Then the crews leaped into longboats and rowed for their own fleet. Behind them, guns exploded one after the other as the flames reached them. To the Spaniards it seemed as if the devil had brought a fleet from hell to fight them.

Panic took over. Spanish sailors cut their anchor cables and tried to escape on the tide. Ships smashed into each other, crushing their hulls. Medina Sidonia kept his head. He refused to abandon his ship, the *San Martin*. He got clear of the entangled galleons and clear of Drake's fireships. He could have escaped. Instead, he dropped anchor and fired a gun to signal for the Armada to return and form around him. It was the act of a good seaman and a brave man. But only a few ships obeyed his signal.

By dawn on Monday, most of the Spanish fleet was adrift off the French town of Gravelines. Medina Sidonia and about fifteen ships faced Admiral Howard and his squadron leaders Drake, Hawkins, Seymour, and Frobisher in the final battle.

Then in the dawn light, Howard saw a huge galleass, the *San Lorenzo*, drifting toward Calais. Its rudder was broken and its admiral, Hugo de Moncada, was pressing his galley slaves to the utmost to row the ship away from the sandy shore. Howard broke away and went after the great prize. Moncada ran aground at the beach in front of Calais Castle. After an hour-long battle, Moncada was killed by a shot between the eyes. Howard ordered his men to tow the great ship, but they couldn't pull it off the sand. They took the treasure chest and everything else they could carry. Then they sailed back to join the rest of the fleet at Gravelines for the final battle.

Medina Sidonia fought bravely. Slowly, the ships that had scattered after the fireship attack gathered around him. After battling the English for seven hours, he had fifty ships, a sizable fighting force. But there was one enemy he could not fight. Once again the weather was against him. A fierce squall struck. The

Armada was strung out along the coast in danger of destruction on the sandbanks. Medina Sidonia watched as his ship came within feet of scraping the bottom and being pounded to pieces. He made his confession and waited for the final surrender.

None of the Englishmen realized the threat from the Armada was over. At the end of the day, Drake wrote a letter to Walsingham. "God hath given us so good a day. . . . Send us munition." He signed it "Your honour's most ready to be commanded, but now half sleeping, Fra. Drake."

Then once again, the wind changed direction. Prayers of thanksgiving rose from the Spanish, and curses from the English. One by one, the Spanish galleons blew northward away from the shore and toward the safety of deep water. The English could do nothing. They needed ammunition and they didn't have it.

The retreat of the Armada

Chapter 10
The Last Voyage

The Armada sailed home to Spain through unfamiliar waters around Scotland and Ireland. Ships sank from battle damage and from storms. They crashed against the coast because they had lost spars and sails. Only half the ships got home.

England suffered its worst losses in the weeks after the fighting, as hundreds of men died from disease. The country was nearly bankrupt from the cost of defense.

Queen Elizabeth wanted the surviving ships of the Armada destroyed before they could attack again. Most of them were in the Spanish port of Santander. She sent Sir Francis Drake as the admiral of the fleet and Sir John Norreys as the general of the land forces. Drake and Norreys had a different plan. They wanted to free Portugal from Spain by helping Don Antonio, one of the claimants to the Portuguese throne. If Don Antonio became king, the Portuguese ports would be open to English trade. England could have a navy base in the Azores and cut off Philip's treasure route.

Drake and Norreys sailed with inexperienced troops, overcrowded ships, and not enough food and supplies. The expedition was poorly planned from the beginning. Drake ignored the port of Santander and went to Corunna. They captured 150 guns, but they didn't take the town.

The next destination was Lisbon. They expected the Portuguese people to rise up and support Don Antonio. But King Philip had a good viceroy in Lisbon, his nephew Archduke Albert. Albert had heard about the battle at Corunna, so he knew that Drake was coming. He rounded up any Portuguese leaders who might support Don Antonio and imprisoned them or hanged them.

Lisbon was a well defended city. Drake had not been able to take it when he stormed Cadiz two years earlier. The Tagus River, whose mouth was at Lisbon, looked wide, but its navigable channel was fairly narrow. It was decided that Norreys and Don Antonio would land at Peniche, forty miles (sixty-four kilometers) away, and march the troops by land to Lisbon. Drake would get past the guns and sail up the Tagus and meet them. When the land force arrived at Lisbon, Drake did not appear. The weather had been too bad for him to sail up the river.

Norreys's men were weak from disease and lack of food. They had no big guns. The peasants did not rise to support Don Antonio. Norreys had to retreat. The expedition went home to England and reported failure. Queen Elizabeth was angry that they had not followed orders and destroyed the ships at Santander. Both Drake and Norreys explained that the wind had been against them, but the queen did not forgive Drake. He did not have another seagoing command for five years.

During this time, Sir Francis Drake served in the House of Commons and spoke often. In Plymouth he carried out a project to give the town a better water supply. The water was taken from a distant river and fed into a leat, or channel, about twenty-seven miles (forty-three kilometers) long. This channel was first

The House of Commons meeting before Queen Elizabeth

opened on April 24, 1591. For years afterward, at the end of April, the town of Plymouth celebrated the Leat Feast. As part of the ceremony, the councillors passed a goblet of water "to the pious memory of Sir Francis Drake." Drake's water project served Plymouth for three hundred years.

Sir John Hawkins wanted to keep a squadron around the Azores to cut off the flow of Spanish treasure, but this wasn't done. As a result, Spain recovered from the Armada and grew stronger. Philip fortified his ports in the New World and built new, modern ships.

In 1595, the queen appointed Drake and Hawkins as joint leaders of an expedition to cut off the treasure. Sir Thomas Baskerville was appointed to lead the land forces. Drake wanted to attack Panama, but the queen was worried about another possible invasion by Spain. She didn't want Drake and Hawkins away from England for more than six months. In August, news came that the flagship of the Spanish treasure fleet had been crippled and was in the port of San Juan, Puerto Rico. The treasure was still aboard. Drake and Hawkins offered to attack San Juan.

For some reason, Drake and Hawkins were unable work cooperatively on this project. Hawkins made careful preparations for provisions of food, medical supplies, even hammocks—the latest thing in comfort. Drake was better at planning small expeditions that lived off the land and took advantage of opportunities. He did not work as well when organizing a large force. He recruited more than his share of men and did not store enough food. Hawkins refused to use his supplies to feed Drake's men. The two raised their voices in argument so much that they gave away their destination and the word got out to the Spaniards.

Drake and Hawkins knew that King Philip was sending a fleet after them. They did not know he had sent five fast frigates to Puerto Rico to rescue the treasure and bring it back to Spain. The frigates caught up to the English ships and captured a small one named the *Francis*. At this point in the voyage, John Hawkins became seriously ill. He died aboard his ship within sight of Puerto Rico. A few hours before he died, he dictated a last message to the queen that he was "old and tired" and saw nothing but ruin for the voyage.

Drake attacked San Juan, but the treasure was safely ashore and the port was heavily defended. Drake backed off in failure and sailed south. He returned to Nombre de Dios, the place of his first great triumph. He captured it easily and landed Baskerville and the soldiers for a march inland. On the old trail, now overgrown jungle, the Spanish ambushed them. After four days, Baskerville gave up and brought his men back to the ship. It was the last day of the year 1595.

One of Drake's officers wrote that, from that moment, "he never carried mirth nor joy in his face." In January Drake became ill with dysentery. He had brought his will with him, and on January 27, 1596, he had it witnessed by six of his friends aboard the *Defiance*. He died early the next morning. He was about fifty-five years old.

Drake's exploits as a sea dog opened the oceans to England. His explorations of the Pacific and his circumnavigation changed the map of the world. His knowledge of ships and naval warfare was critical in modernizing the English navy. His genius as a military leader in the battle with the Armada saved his country from the greatest threat it had ever faced.

Drake's greatness can be measured in another way. He treated the common sailors and Spanish prisoners with respect and compassion. In the journals of the crews and the testimony of Spaniards before the Inquisition, their admiration shines through the pages across four hundred years.

Sir Francis Drake was buried at sea. It was a fitting place for a man who had lived on ships since childhood and had hardly ever walked on land.

His death marked the end of an age. Sir Francis Drake had written his name across the map of the world, and his grateful country would remember him forever.

Portrait of "Francis Drake, most noble English knight. He it is who circumnavigated the whole earth."

Appendix

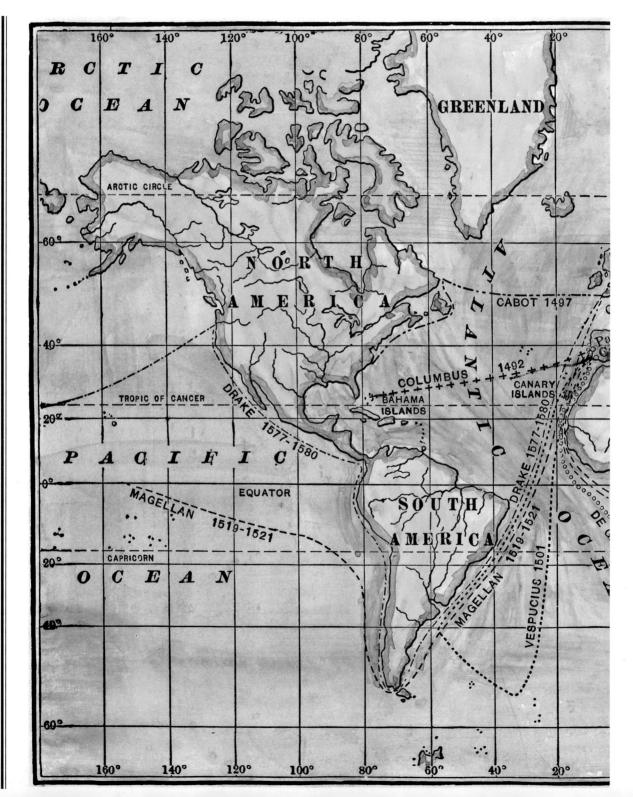

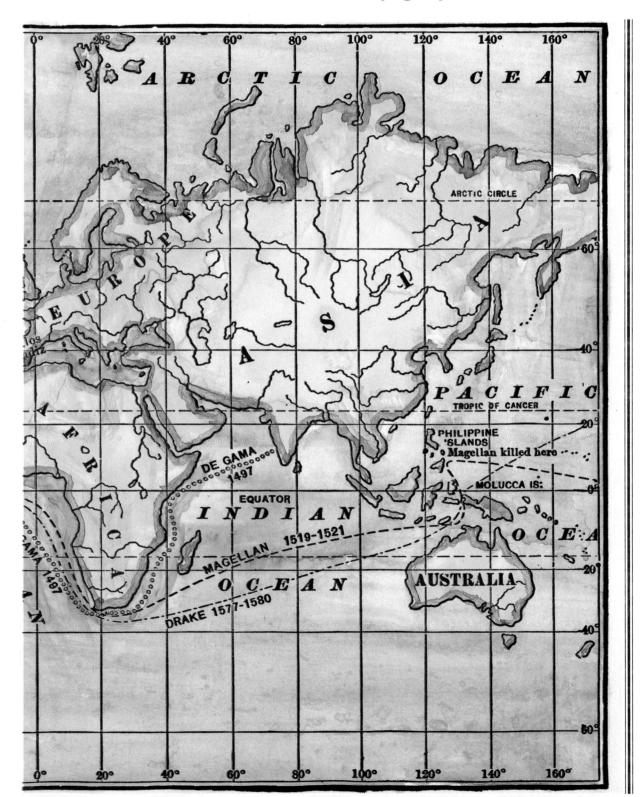

Timeline of Events in Drake's Lifetime

1540?—Francis Drake is born on Crowndale Farm at Tavistock near Plymouth, England

1547—King Henry VIII dies and Edward VI becomes king of England

1549—The Church of England's *Book of Common Prayer* is published; Catholics rebel; the Drakes, as Protestant refugees, flee Tavistock and move into an abandoned ship in on the Medway River in Kent

1553—Edward VI dies; Mary becomes queen of England and marries Philip II of Spain

Around 1555—Francis Drake goes to work on a boat traveling the English Channel and the North Sea to Zeeland

1558—Queen Mary dies and Elizabeth becomes queen of England

1562-1563—John Hawkins makes his first slaving voyage

1566—Drake sails with John Lovell on a slaving venture to the Spanish West Indies

1567—Drake commands the *Judith* on a slaving mission with John Hawkins to the West Indies

1568—Drake and Hawkins take part in the Battle of San Juan de Ulúa off the coast of Mexico; the Netherlands rebels against Spain

1569—Drake marries Mary Newman

1570 and 1571—Drake makes two information-gathering expeditions to the Caribbean

1572—Drake voyages to the Caribbean to raid Spanish treasure trains at Nombre de Dios, Panama; he enlists the aid of the Cimaroons, a group of Africans who escaped slavery under the Spaniards

1573—Drake captures a shipment of gold bound for Nombre de Dios; he is the first Englishman to see the Pacific Ocean

1577—Drake begins his voyage that circumnavigates the globe; John Hawkins is appointed treasurer of the navy

1580—Drake returns to Plymouth after sailing around the world; Spain annexes Portugal

1581—Drake is knighted aboard the *Golden Hind* and made mayor of Plymouth; he buys Buckland Abbey

1583—Drake's wife Mary dies

1584—Drake is elected to the House of Commons in Parliament

1585—Drake marries Elizabeth Sydenham; he captures Santo Domingo and Cartagena in the West Indies

1587—Drake leads an attack on Spain and destroys more than twenty Spanish ships in Cadiz harbor

1588—The Spanish Armada sets sail for England; Drake, vice admiral under Admiral Howard, helps battle the fleet in the English Channel

1589—Commanding 150 ships, Drake leads an unsuccessful attack on Lisbon, Portugal

1595—Drake sails with John Hawkins on another voyage to the West Indies; Hawkins dies at sea near San Juan, Puerto Rico

1596—Francis Drake dies aboard the *Defiance* on January 28 and is buried at sea

Glossary of Terms

arbitration—The settling of disputes using an outside party

artillery—Guns, cannons, and other weapons that shoot explosives

autopsy—An examination of a corpse to determine the cause of death

ballast—Something heavy put in a ship to make it stable in the water

broadsides—Shots fired from all the guns on the side of a ship

bullion—A mass of gold or silver

caravel—A small, wide ship with a high rear deck

carrack—A broad-beamed (wide) cargo ship

cartographer—Mapmaker

charade—False, insincere, or misleading actions

circumnavigate—To sail all the way around something

coffer—A treasury or chest of money

cooper—A person who makes or repairs wooden barrels

dispatch—An important message sent by a military or naval officer

dry dock—An area where ships are cleaned and repaired

Dutch—Relating to the Netherlands

dysentery—An intestinal infection causing diarrhea

factions—Groups that hold opposing views

flagship—The ship in a fleet that carries the commander

founder—To weaken, become crippled, collapse, or sink

frigate—A narrow, swift, square-sailed ship powered by oars

galleass—A large ship powered by both sails and oars

galleon—A square-sailed ship of the 1400s through 1700s, used for war or trade

galley slaves—Slaves who row the oars that propel a ship

heresy—A belief that is contrary to a church's official teachings

heretic—A person who holds a belief that is a heresy

indulgences—Promises that punishment for sins will be removed in return for saying certain prayers, doing good deeds, or donating money

hold—The cargo-stowing area of a ship

interrogate—To question

jettisoned—Thrown overboard to make a ship lighter

labyrinth—A confusing maze of unfamiliar pathways

longboat—A long rowboat carried on a sailing ship

looting—Seizing goods from a defeated enemy

massacre—A brutal, bloody battle

merchantman—A merchant ship

monopoly—Total control of something by just one person or group

moor—To anchor a ship or tie it to something on shore

Moors—Muslims from North Africa who conquered Spain in the eighth century

omen—An event or sign that seems to predict a future event

page—A young boy in training to be a knight

parliament—The lawmaking body of Great Britain and some other countries

pestilence—An infectious disease that sweeps over a large area

pinnace—A small, light vessel with sails and oars

plunder—Loot taken by force in wartime

privateer—A private ship appointed to attack enemy cargo ships or warships

Protestant—Member of a church that originated by pulling away from the Catholic Church in protest of some of its teachings

quoit of gold—A flat disk of gold

reinforcements—Extra supplies, equipment, or people needed for an operation

sacrilege—An outrageously irreverent act

scimitar—A sword with a wide, curved blade

silhouetted—Appearing as a dark figure in an outlined form

sorcery—The use of evil spirits or magic

spar—A long, rounded piece of wood to support a ship's rigging

spoils—Goods taken in war

squadron—As a naval term, an organized group of ships

squall—A violent rainstorm

standard—A flag or banner representing the king or queen

stern—The rear end of a boat

steward—A sailor who is in charge of the ship's food and other support services

ton—(The size of a ship was given in terms of tons. The figure was an estimate. In Drake's time, a "ton" or "tun" was a barrel that held 252 gallons of wine. So a 100-ton ship was one that could carry about 100 barrels of wine in its hold.)

treachery—Betrayal of trust or confidence

treason—An attempt to damage or overthrow one's government

tropics—Warm areas of the earth near the equator

truce—An agreement to stop fighting

vengeance—Actions taken for revenge or to get even

vicar—A minister in charge of a mission or parish

Bibliography

Most of these books about Francis Drake are adult books that older students may enjoy. Those suitable for younger readers are indicated as such in parentheses.

Bradford, Ernle D. S. *The Wind Commands Me: A Life of Sir Francis Drake.* NY: Harcourt, Brace & World, 1965.

Drake, Francis. *The World Encompassed by Sir Francis Drake.* W. S. Vaux, editor. NY: Burt Franklin. Reprint of 1854 edition.

Gibbs, Lewis. *The Silver Circle.* London: J. M. Dent and Sons,1963.

Goodnough, David. *Francis Drake.* Mahwah, NJ: Troll Associates, 1979. (For younger readers)

Hampden, John, editor. *Francis Drake, Privateer: Contemporary Narratives and Documents.* University, AL: University of Alabama Press, 1972.

Hook, Jason. *Sir Francis Drake.* NY: Bookwright Press, 1988. (For younger readers)

Latham, Jean Lee. *Drake, the Man They Called a Pirate.* NY: Harper, 1960. (For younger readers)

Roche, Thomas William Edgar. *The Golden Hind.* NY: Praeger, 1973.

Syme, Ronald. *Francis Drake, Sailor of the Unknown Seas.* NY: Morrow, 1961. (For younger readers)

Thomson, George M. *Sir Francis Drake.* NY: William Morrow, 1972.

Williamson, James A. *Sir Francis Drake.* Westport, CN: Greenwood, 1975. Reprint of 1951 edition.

Wilson, Derek A. *The World Encompassed: Francis Drake and His Great Voyage.* NY: Harper & Row, 1977.

Index

Page numbers in boldface type indicate illustrations.

Picture Identifications for Chapter Opening Spreads

6-7—The harbor at Calais, France
10-11—The English countryside in Kent
22-23—Cartagena, on the Spanish Main
32-33—The Caribbean coast of Panama near Portobello
44-45—Old Spanish mule trail across the Isthmus of Panama
58-59—Seagulls and fjords off the southern coast of Chile
74-75—Drake's Bay at Point Reyes National Seashore, California
86-87—Skyline of Cadiz, Spain
98-99—The Spanish Armada
112-113—Sundown in the coastal area of Hispaniola

Picture Acknowledgments

Steven Gaston Dobson—Cover illustration

© Joan Dunlop—103

© Victor Englebert—27

© Virginia R. Grimes—74-75, 82

Historical Pictures Service, Chicago—2, 9, 12 (margin), 13, 14, 21, 22-23, 48, 60 (2 pictures), 62, 63, 68, 73, 80, 85, 89, 91, 93, 104, 106, 108, 117

Courtesy of Library of Congress—71

© Buddy Mays/Travel Stock—10-11, 94 (bottom), 95, 112-113

North Wind Picture Archives—6-7, 18 (2 pictures), 19, 20 (2 pictures), 31, 35, 39, 40, 43, 53, 54, 57, 64, 67, 69, 70, 78, 83, 90, 92, 97, 101, 102, 109, 111, 114, 118-119

Odyssey Productions: © Robert Frerck—32-33, 44-45, 86-87, 94 (top)

© Chip and Rosa Maria Peterson—50, 58-59

H. Armstrong Roberts—5

© Bob and Ira Spring—4, 25

SuperStock—12 (top), 16, 17, 88, 98-99

Valan Photos: © Jean-Marie Jro—49; © Y.R.Tymstra—79; © Wouterloot-Gregoire—76

About the Author

Roberta Bard was born in New York City, grew up in New Jersey, and has lived most of her adult life in the Chicago area. She received a B.A. in political science from Northwestern University and an M.A. in social work from the University of Chicago. Ms. Bard always loved history, she says, "because they told you such good stories. It wasn't like arithmetic." She also writes mysteries and song lyrics. She is married to Warren Ruby and has a son, David.